Best of *Bead&Button* magazine

Peyote Stitch Beading Projects

Compiled by Julia Gerlach

Printed in the United States of America

05 06 07 08 09 10 11 12 13 14   10 9 8 7 6 5 4 3 2 1

Publisher's Cataloging-In-Publication Data
(Prepared by The Donohue Group, Inc.)

Peyote stitch projects : from the pages of Bead & button magazine.

    p. : ill. ; cm. -- (Best of Bead & button magazine)
  Includes index.
  ISBN: 0-87116-218-0

1. Beadwork--Patterns. 2. Beadwork--Handbooks, manuals, etc. I. Title: Bead & button.

TT860 .P49 2005
745.582

Managing Art Director: Lisa Bergman
Photographers: Jim Forbes, William Zuback
Project editors: Julia Gerlach, Pam O'Connor

Acknowledgements: Mindy Brooks, Terri Field, Lora Groszkiewicz, Kellie Jaeger, Diane Jolie, Patti Keipe, Alice Korach, Tonya Limberg, Debbie Nishihara, Cheryl Phelan, Carrie Rohloff, Carole Ross, Candice St. Jacques, Maureen Schimmel, Lisa Schroeder, Terri Torbeck, Elizabeth Weber, Lesley Weiss

These designs are for your personal use. They are not intended for resale.
All projects have appeared previously in *Bead&Button* magazine.

CONTENTS

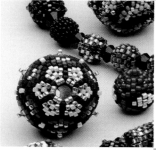

INTRODUCTION

When *Bead&Button* magazine began publication in 1994, a period of exuberant discovery and experimentation had begun in the bead community. Interest in traditional beadwork had revealed to a new generation of bead artists a wonderful array of off-loom beadweaving stitches from American Indian, African, Russian, and other cultures. With enthusiasm, artists began to adopt these techniques to make innovative works of art and ornamentation.

Breakthrough works such as Virginia Blakelock's Cellini spiral necklaces (demonstrated by Deb Samuels on page 46) and Wendy Ellsworth's rapid-increase peyote-stitch vessels (page 90) expanded everyone's conception of what was possible. These and many other novel applications of traditional techniques were first introduced to the world at large through the pages of *Bead&Button*.

Peyote stitch, sometimes called gourd stitch, is a beadweaving technique adapted from Native American traditional beadwork. Many bead artists consider it foremost among their creative tools. It creates a sinuous fabric by closely nestling the beads next to each other. When a highly uniform type of cylinder bead was introduced to the American market by Japanese bead companies Miyuki and Toho, the tight weave of peyote stitch took on a new relevance. Artists could create sleek, glittering surfaces that exactly rendered charted designs. These beads gave a centuries-old stitch a new-millennium look.

Within these pages, you will find works that draw from the rich traditions of the past and those that look to the future. Selected from 11 years of publication, the very best designs have been included in these pages: beautiful jewelry, bags, and objects that make this traditional stitch supremely relevant for today's bead artist.

Several of these projects are expressly oriented to the process of peyote stitching, providing techniques and methods to help you devise your own version of the work—with the benefit of the artist's expertise. Others give you step-by-step guidance for replicating a piece of jewelry or artwork.

Whichever road you take, you'll appreciate the many resources *Bead&Button* consistently provides: a comprehensive "Basics" section, detailed materials lists, clear how-to photographs and figures, and the confidence that all our projects have been tested by the editors. Take some time to browse through our "Gallery" section for inspiration and then get started on your own peyote pursuit.

– The editors of Bead&Button

BASICS

CONDITIONING THREAD

Conditioning straightens and strengthens your thread and also helps it resist fraying, separating, and tangling. Pull unwaxed nylon threads like Nymo through either beeswax (not candle wax or paraffin) or Thread Heaven to condition. Beeswax adds tackiness that is useful if you want your beadwork to fit tightly. Thread Heaven adds a static charge that causes the thread to repel itself, so it can't be used with doubled thread. All nylon threads stretch, so maintain tension on the thread as you condition it.

HALF-HITCH KNOT

Come out a bead and form a loop perpendicular to the thread between beads. Bring the needle under the thread away from the loop. Then go back over the thread and through the loop. Pull gently so the knot doesn't tighten prematurely.

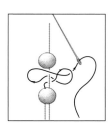

OVERHAND KNOT

Make a loop and pass the working end through it. Pull the ends to tighten the knot.

SQUARE KNOT

1 Cross the left-hand cord over the right-hand cord, and then bring it under the right-hand cord from back to front. Pull it up in front so both ends are facing upwards.

2 Cross right over left, forming a loop, and go through the loop, again from back to front. Pull the ends to tighten the knot.

SURGEON'S KNOT

Cross the right end over the left and go through loop. Go through loop again. Pull ends to tighten. Cross the left end over the right and go through once. Tighten.

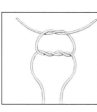

LADDER AND BRICK STITCH

1 A ladder of seed or bugle beads is most often used to begin brick stitch: Pick up two beads. Leave a 3-4-in. (8-10cm) tail and go through both beads again in the same direction. Pull the top bead down so the beads are side by side. The thread exits the bottom of bead #2. String bead #3 and go back through #2 from top to bottom. Come back up #3.

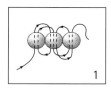

2 String bead #4. Go through #3 from bottom to top and #4 from top to bottom. Add odd-numbered beads like #3 and even-numbered beads like #4.

3 To stabilize the ladder, zigzag back through all the beads.

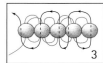

4 Begin each row so no thread shows on the edge: String two beads. Go under the thread between the second and third beads on the ladder from back to front. Pull tight. Go up the second bead added, then down the first. Come back up the second bead.

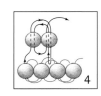

5 For the remaining stitches on each row, pick up one bead. Pass the needle under the next loop on the row below from back to front. Go back up the new bead.

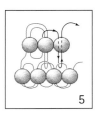

EVEN-COUNT FLAT PEYOTE

1 String one bead and loop through it again in the same direction (remove the extra loop and weave the tail into the work after a few rows). String beads to total an even number. In peyote stitch, rows are nestled together and counted diagonally, so these beads actually comprise the first two rows.

2 To begin row 3 (the numbers in the drawings below indicate rows), pick up a bead and stitch through the second bead from the end. Pick up a bead and go through the fourth bead from the end. Continue in this manner. End by going through the first bead strung.

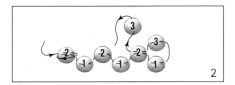

3 To start row 4 and all other rows, pick up a bead and go through the last bead added on the previous row.

To end a thread, weave through the work in a zigzag path, tying two half-hitch knots (see p. 5) along the way. Go through a few more beads before trimming the thread close to the work. To resume stitching, anchor a new thread in the work with half-hitch knots, zigzag through the work, and exit the last bead added in the same direction. Continue stitching where you left off.

EVEN-COUNT CIRCULAR PEYOTE

1 String an even number of beads to equal the desired circumference. Tie in a circle, leaving some ease.

2 Even-numbered beads form row 1 and odd-numbered beads, row 2. (Numbers indicate rows.) Put the ring over a form if desired. Go through the first bead to the left of the knot. Pick up a bead (#1 of row 3), skip a bead, and go through the next bead. Repeat around until you're back to the start.

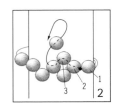

3 Since you started with an even number of beads, you need to work a "step up" to be in position for the next row. Go through the first beads on rows 2 and 3. Pick up a bead and go through the second bead of row 3; continue.

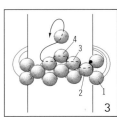

ODD-COUNT CIRCULAR PEYOTE

Start as for circular even-count steps 1-2 above. However, when you begin with an odd number of beads, there won't be a step up; you'll keep spiraling.

PEYOTE STITCH RAPID INCREASE

1 At the point of the increase, pick up two beads instead of one. Pass the needle through the next bead.

2 When you reach the double bead space on the next row, go through the first bead, add a bead, and go through the second bead.

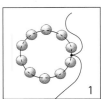

PEYOTE STITCH GRADUAL INCREASE

1 The gradual increase takes four rows. At the point of the increase, pick up two thin beads. Go through the next high bead.

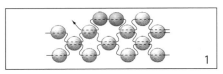

2 When you get to the two thin beads on row 2, go through them as if they were one bead.

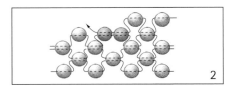

3 On row 3, place two regular-size beads in the two-thin-bead space.

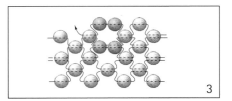

4 When you get to the two beads on the next row, go through the first, pick up a bead, and go through the second.

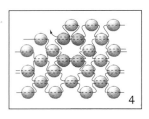

PEYOTE STITCH RAPID DECREASE

1 At the point of the decrease, don't pick up a bead. Instead, go through two beads on the previous row.

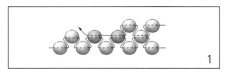

2 When you reach the point where you went through two beads, pick up one bead; continue peyote stitch.

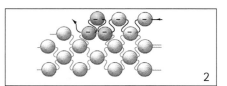

TWO-DROP PEYOTE STITCH

Work two-drop peyote stitch just like peyote stitch, but treat every pair of beads as if it were a single bead.

1 Start with an even number of beads divisible by four. Pick up two beads, skip the first two beads, and go through the next two beads. Repeat across, ending by going through the last two beads.

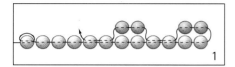

2 Pick up two beads and go through the last two beads added. Repeat across the row. To end, go through the first two beads added on the previous row. Continue adding rows to reach the desired length.

JOINING PEYOTE PIECES

To join two sections of a flat peyote piece invisibly, begin with a high bead on one side and a low bead on the other. Go through each high bead, alternating sides.

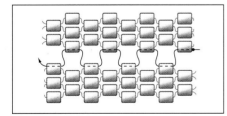

SQUARE STITCH

1 String the required number of beads for the first row. Then string the first bead of the second row and go through the last bead of the first row and the first bead of the second row in the same direction. The new bead sits on top of the old bead and the holes are horizontal.

2 String the second bead of row 2 and go through the next-to-last bead of row 1. Continue through the new bead of row 2. Repeat this step for the entire row.

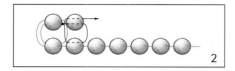

SPIRAL ROPE

A spiral rope is formed by stitching a shorter row of "outer" beads around a longer row of "inner" beads. The tension between the two rows is what causes the beads to twist.

These instructions show how to make spiral rope with two sizes of beads: size 8°s for the inner beads and size 11°s for the outer beads. You may also use beads of a single size, like all 11°s. In that case, you would string fewer beads for the outer beads (i.e. four beads for the inner row and three for the outer row).

1 String four 8° and four 11° seed beads, leaving an 8-in. (20cm) tail.

2 Go through the four 8°s again in the same direction.

3 String an 8° and four 11°s. Go through the last three 8°s of the previous stitch and the 8° just added. Keep the tension firm as you work. Each new loop of beads should sit on top of the previous one. Repeat until you reach the desired length.

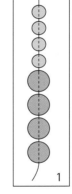

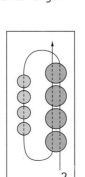

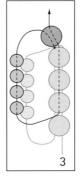

TWO-BEAD BACKSTITCH

1 Thread a needle and decide which area to bead first. Tie a very small knot at the end of the thread. To attach the thread to the fabric, sew into the fabric two bead lengths from the beginning of a beading line. Sew up through the fabric at the beginning of the beading line.

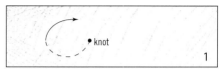

2 To start beaded backstitch, string two beads and lay them along the line of beading on the fabric. Sew down through the fabric right in front of the second bead. Bead straight lines until you're comfortable with the stitch.

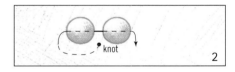

3 Sew up through the fabric between the two beads. Carefully tighten the stitch by giving the thread a little pull where it emerges from the fabric. Do not pull too hard or the material will pucker. Now go through the second bead in the same direction.

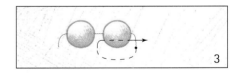

4 Repeat steps 2-3, continuing to follow the beading line. To end a thread, sew into the fabric after the last bead. Sew up between the third and fourth bead from the end. Knot around the thread between the third and fourth beads. Go through a few beads in the beaded line and knot again. Go through a few more beads, pull on the thread slightly and trim close to the beads.

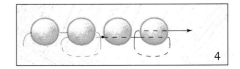

FLATTENED CRIMP

1 Hold the crimp bead using the tip of your chainnose pliers. Squeeze the pliers firmly to flatten the crimp. Tug the clasp to make sure the crimp has a solid grip on the wire. If the wire slides, remove the crimp bead and repeat the steps with a new crimp bead.
2 The flattened crimp should be secure.

FOLDED CRIMP

1 Position the crimp bead in the notch closest to the crimping pliers' handle.
2 Separate the wires and firmly squeeze the crimp.

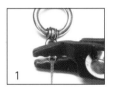 

3 Move the crimp into the notch at the pliers' tip and hold the crimp as shown. Squeeze the crimp bead, folding it in half at the indentation.
4 The folded crimp should be secure.

JUMP RINGS

1 Hold the jump ring with two pairs of chainnose pliers or chainnose and roundnose pliers, as shown.
2 To open the jump ring, angle the tips of one pair of pliers toward you and angle the other pair of tips away.

3 Reverse the steps to close the open jump ring.

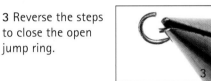

WRAPPED LOOP

1 Make sure you have at least 1¼ in. (3.2cm) of wire above the bead. With the tip of your chainnose pliers, grasp the wire directly above the bead. Bend the wire (above the pliers) into a right angle.
2 Using roundnose pliers, position the jaws vertically in the bend.

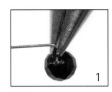 

3 Bring the wire over the top jaw of the roundnose pliers.
4 Keep the jaws vertical and reposition the pliers' lower jaw snugly into the loop. Curve the wire downward around the bottom of the roundnose pliers. This is the first half of a wrapped loop.

5 Position the chainnose pliers' jaws across the loop.
6 Wrap the wire around the wire stem, covering the stem between the loop and the top bead. Trim the excess wire and press the cut end close to the wraps with chainnose pliers.

 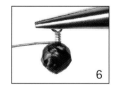

GALLERY

Gathered peyote purse by Carol Kaplan

Peyote ornament by Karen Boylan

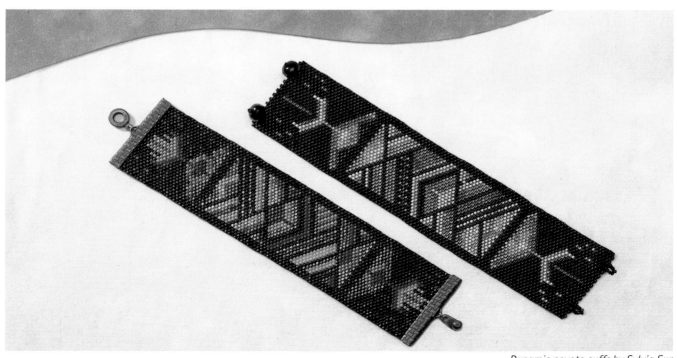

Dynamic peyote cuffs by Sylvia Sur

Peyote stitch beaded handbag by Karen Boylan

Triple-tube peyote bracelets by Ava Farrington

GALLERY

Bezeled computer circuit necklace by Laura Jean McCabe

Beaded pillbox hat by Leah Kabaker

Peyote ornament cover by Deb Moffett-Hall

Imperial Chinese robe by Sharmini Wirasekara

Beaded needle cases by Karen L. Whitney

Wildflower purse by Susan Hillyer

JEWELRY

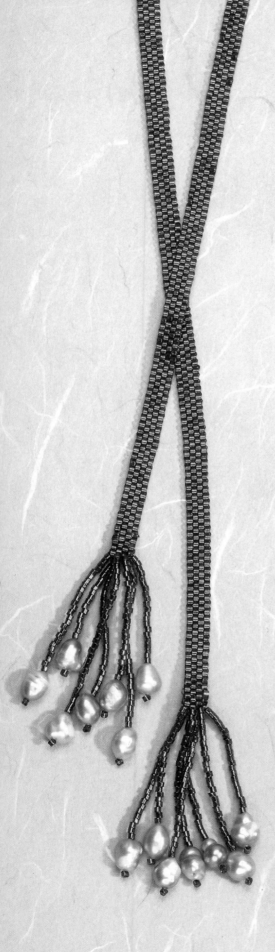

Peyote ribbon lariat

If you've never done peyote stitch before, this thin, slinky lariat will make a satisfying first project. With each row being only two beads wide, you'll progress quickly, yet the final product is impressive. The dangles on the ends provide additional substance and flair.

For a smooth, flat ribbon, use Japanese cylinder beads, as shown here. Or make a lariat with a more textured surface by using Czech seed beads. This lariat is perfectly plain—all in one color —but if you'd prefer a pattern, by all means add one. Feel free to vary the number of stitches in your row, but stick with an even number of beads to keep your project as simple as possible.

Work a ribbon of two-bead-wide flat peyote 4-5 ft. (1.2-1.5m) long. Add six to eight dangles on each end. You can wear the necklace as a very long tied rope (it would also make a fun belt). Alternatively, double it and pass both ends through the fold at the front; or center it on the front of your neck, cross the ends behind your neck, and then tie them together in front.

❶ Start with a 1½-2-yd. (1.4-1.8m) length of single thread on a needle. Tie a stop bead about 6 in. (15cm) from the end (you'll take it off and weave the tail in later).

❷ String four cylinder beads for rows 1 and 2. Work in even-count flat peyote (see "Basics," p. 5) until about 4-6 in. (10-15cm) of thread remains.

❸ To add new thread, thread another needle with Nymo and weave it into the beadwork, making a few half-hitch knots as you go (see "Basics"). Exit the high bead at the edge with the needle pointing toward the ribbon and resume

peyote stitch. When you've worked several rows, weave in the tail of the previous thread, making a few half-hitch knots, the same way you started the new thread. Then trim both tails.

❹ Keep adding new threads as needed until the ribbon is 4-5 ft. long.

❺ To add the dangles, weave a 36-in. (.9m)-long doubled thread into the end of the ribbon and string 1-2 in. (2.5-5cm) of cylinder beads. String a pearl and a final cylinder bead. Go back up through the pearl and all the cylinder beads and exit the next bead on the end (photo). String a total of six to eight fringes of slightly different lengths. You can put two fringes in the same space between end beads. Then weave the thread into the ribbon and make a few half-hitch knots before clipping it close. Repeat at the other end.
– Louise Malcolm

MATERIALS

- 20g size 11º Japanese cylinder beads
- 12–16 pearls or other beads for fringe
- Nymo B beading thread
- beeswax or Thread Heaven
- beading needles, #12

Easy peyote tube

If you want to learn circular peyote stitch, this is a great first project. Created in odd-count peyote with three colors of large beads, it is eye-catching, fashionable, and versatile. Odd-count circular peyote stitch with large beads is the easiest form of circular peyote because the rows have no distinct end. They just continue spiraling (see "Basics," p. 5).

String the tube onto a satin cord for an alluringly simple necklace. After you make the first one, try some of the variations that are suggested on page 16 or try some of your own ideas.

PEYOTE STITCH TUBE

❶ Thread a needle with a comfortable length of doubled beading cord. Sew through a contrast-color stop bead twice, leaving a 9-in. (23cm) tail.

❷ Pick up seven beads in the following order: two color A, two color B, two color C, and one color A. Slide them to the stop bead. Go through the first bead again to close the circle (photo a). Be careful to not split the thread when going back through a bead. When starting a tube, it helps to put it on a chopstick, dowel, or other form to keep the beadwork tight so you can position new beads correctly. Keep the new row near the tip of the chopstick. Maintain tension by keeping the cord taut between two fingers of the hand holding the chopstick.

❸ Pick up one A bead, skip the next bead on the circle, and go through the

a

b

c

f

d

g

e

h

off onto the other end of the tube so the necklace is still the desired length.

8 To finish, tie a half-hitch knot between the last bead and its neighbor. Go through all the beads at this end of the tube at least once **(photo g)** and knot to the body thread again. Weave back along the thread path as in step 6 to end the thread.

9 Repeat step 8 to end the starting tail in the same manner.

FINISHING

1 Use a piece of wire as a harness to string the tube onto satin cord. Cut a piece of craft wire more than twice the length of the tube. Double it and feed the folded end through the tube, being careful not to come through the beadwork. Thread the satin cord through the folded end and pull it back through the tube **(photo h)**. Pull one end of the cord out and center the tube on the cord.

2 Use large-hole beads for decorative dangles. Pass the cord through the bead and tie an overhand knot (see "Basics") at the end of the cord. Snug the bead up against the knot and repeat on the other side of the bead. Repeat on the other end of the cord.

VARIATIONS

Vary color, size, or type of bead for different effects. Start with five beads if you use size 5º. For lengthwise stripes, use different colors on the first row, then match the color to the bead below as you work. Changing colors after several rows will make horizontal stripes. Size 5º triangle beads align flat-side out. Drop-shaped beads interlock with the bulb-end showing for a nubby texture. – *Samantha Lynn*

MATERIALS
- size 6º seed beads, 10g in each of three colors
- 2 large-hole beads for dangles
- beading needles or sharps, #8 or 10
- Strfingth bead cord, size 1-3, or nylon upholstery thread
- 40 in. (1m) 1mm satin cord/rattail
- 26-gauge craft wire
- clear nail polish or G-S Hypo Cement

Optional: chopstick or dowel

third bead **(photo b, p.15)**. Pick up a B bead, skip the next bead on the circle, and go through the fifth bead. Pick up a C bead, skip the next bead on the circle, and go through the next bead, which is the last bead on the first round.

4 Pick up one A bead and go through the first bead added in round 2 **(photo c)**.

5 Continue in this fashion, adding one bead per color in each round to form spirals of color **(photo d)**. Discard malformed beads. Don't worry about tension at first. After the third round, give the working thread a gentle tug to snug the beads together. From now on, it will be obvious where each new bead goes, and the tension will take care of itself. When the tube is long enough to hold, you may put the chopstick aside if you wish.

6 If you need to add thread, thread a new needle and go through two or three beads two rows back, working toward the old needle. Tie a half-hitch knot (see **photo e** and "Basics"). Follow the old thread path through a few more beads and tie another half-hitch knot. Repeat two more times, ending with the new needle exiting the same bead as the old needle **(photo f)**. Resume work with the new needle. After working a few rows, take the old thread through a few beads and tie a half-hitch knot. Repeat at least twice. End by going through a few beads before cutting off the thread. Dot the knots with glue applied from the tip of the needle.

7 When you reach the desired length for your necklace, untie the stop bead. Gently pick off the first few rounds of beads until you reach stitches with firm tension. Work the beads you've picked

Alternative circular peyote start

Beginning beaders sometimes get frustrated with circular peyote stitch at first because they experience the "Barbie Skirt" syndrome. They put what seems to be the right number of beads around a form and begin stitching only to find the work soon flaring out. What they end up with is a beautifully beaded skirt fit for a Barbie doll.

To prevent this from happening, remember to remove half the beads from the foundation row. This creates the space into which you will weave the second row. Here's what to do:

❶ Measure the form you'll be beading around by wrapping a string of beads around it **(photo a)**. Then remove half of them. For example, for a 50-bead pattern, begin with 25 beads. If your initial round of beads is an uneven number, add one more. (If the tube is too loose, you can break a bead out of row 2 later on.)

Note: If you're using this method to begin a project with a predetermined bead count for the foundation row, first string the specified number of beads. Then, make a form to bead around by cutting a toilet paper roll lengthwise, bringing it in to fit in the circle of beads, and taping it. Then remove half the beads as indicated above.

❷ Run the needle through all the beads again to form a circle, and place the circle over your form an inch or two down from the top **(photo b).** As you work, keep going in the same direction as the thread.

❸ The secret to a solid foundation row is holding onto the tail (tape helps). Use your thumb to hold it snugly to the form and put the needle through one bead to lock the row in **(photo c)**. Tighten it by pulling on the tail and working thread.

❹ Pick up one bead and go through the next bead on the foundation row

a

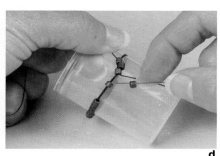

d

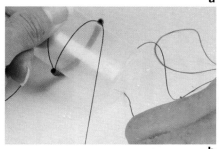

b

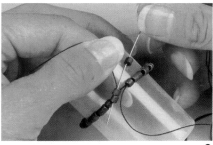

e

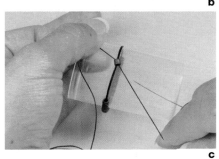

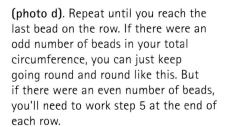

c

(photo d). Repeat until you reach the last bead on the row. If there were an odd number of beads in your total circumference, you can just keep going round and round like this. But if there were an even number of beads, you'll need to work step 5 at the end of each row.

❺ Pick up one bead and go through the last bead of the foundation row (the bead you went through in photo c) then go through the first bead of the second row. This is called the "step-up." If you lose your step-up, you have increased one bead. That's where people tend to go wrong. – *Nicole Campanella*

Embellished peyote tube necklace

If you love the look of beaded ropes but don't want to crochet one, try making these peyote tubes and embellishing them with a picot trim. The basic tube is easy to stitch, and the picot variations seem limitless. This tube is done in even-count circular peyote, so you'll learn the "step up" that's necessary to start a new row.

Consider using anywhere from four to ten beads for the tube's circumference and work with different bead sizes, shapes, and colors. Once the tube is done, it's ready for decoration. Keep it simple with a single row of three-bead picot or take out your bead stash and have fun.

❶ To make a peyote tube, string eight or more (use an even number) main color beads on 2 yd. (1.8m) of conditioned Nymo and slide the beads close to the tail. Knot the tail and working thread together with a surgeon's knot (see "Basics," p. 5),

forming a ring. Leave a little slack between beads.

❷ Sew through the bead after the knot. Pick up a bead, skip a bead, and go through the next bead (photo a). Repeat around the circle, working in even-count circular peyote (see "Basics"). To start the next row, step up by going through the last bead of the previous row and the first of the current row.

❸ Work in circular peyote until your necklace is the desired length. Sew through a bead or two in the last row before starting the picots.

❹ To add the picot trim, pick up three accent color beads and go though the bead that's next along the spiral (photo b). Follow a single line of spiraling beads as you stitch. When you reach the other end of the necklace, bury the thread tails in the beadwork. Make a second picot spiral alongside the first, if desired.

❺ Secure an 18-in. (46cm) length of

beading cord in the last few rows with two or three half-hitch knots (see "Basics") between beads. String a bead cap, go through the loop on the clasp, then go back through the bead cap (photo c). Sew through a few beads in the end row and repeat at least two more times for stability. Secure the cord in the beadwork with half-hitch knots. Finish the other end to match.

– Debbie Phillips

MATERIALS

- 25g size 11º seed beads, main color
- 25g size 11º seed beads, accent color
- 2 bead caps
- clasp
- Nymo D beading thread
- beeswax or Thread Heaven
- 1 yd. (.9m) Strength, Fireline fishing line, or other beading cord
- beading needles, #10

Two- & three-drop peyote bracelet

Combining different sizes and types of beads can be a fun way to make an interesting item. For this bracelet, make use of two- and three-drop peyote to showcase Miyuki square beads in a band of Delicas. The square beads are the same size as a three-drop peyote stitch. Work single peyote around the square. Then, to add more textural interest, use two-drop peyote on the outer edge of the bracelet. If you want to add more contrast, you can use different color Delicas to frame the square bead.

This bracelet works up quickly, but you should be comfortable working in two- and three-drop peyote before you begin.

SOLID-COLOR ROWS

Condition beading thread (see "Basics," p. 5) at a length that you find most comfortable. Determine the desired finished length of your bracelet. The beaded portion of this bracelet is 6½ in. (16cm). The closure adds another ½ in. (1.3cm).

❶ Leaving a 4-5-in. (10-12cm) tail, pick up 11 main color (MC) Delicas. Skip the last four beads strung and go through the next bead (photo a and figure 1, a–b). The last two beads strung sit above the eighth and ninth beads strung to form a new row. You may have to adjust the beads so they sit correctly.

❷ Pick up three MCs. Skip three beads and go through the next bead. This makes a three-drop peyote stitch. Then pick up two MC (photo b).

❸ Sew through all the beads in the

a

b

figure 1

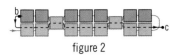

figure 2

figure 3

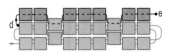

figure 4

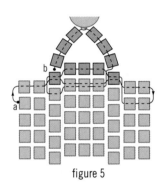

figure 5

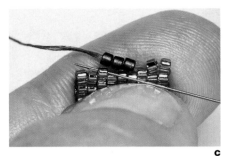

c

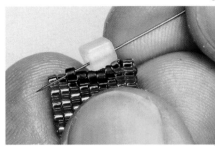

d

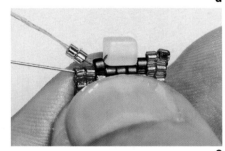

e

f

MATERIALS

- 5g Japanese cylinder beads (Delicas), main color (MC)
- 1g Japanese cylinder beads (Delicas), accent color (AC)
- 11-13 Miyuki square beads, size 3
- Nymo or Power Pro beading cord in matching color
- beading needles, #10
- beeswax or Thread Heaven for Nymo
- magnetic clasp
- safety chain and 2 jump rings

Tools: chainnose pliers

❷ Use pliers to open a jump ring (see "Basics"). Slide it onto the magnetic clasp's loop. Then slide an end link of the safety chain into the ring. Close the loop **(photo f)**. Repeat on the other end of the bracelet. – *Rae Ann Wojahn*

previous row **(figure 2, b–c)** exiting the last bead. Repeat this step every other row for the entire bracelet.

❹ Go through the first two beads in the next row and pick up one MC. Sew through the next three beads, and pick up one MC. Go through the next two beads **(figure 3, c–d)**.

❺ Pick up two MC and go through the next bead. This completes a two-drop stitch. Work a three-drop, and then a two-drop **(figure 4, d–e)**.

❻ Repeat steps 4-5 to work four solid-color rows.

SQUARE-BEAD MOTIF

❶ Begin the next row with a MC two-drop. Then work an accent color (AC) three-drop **(photo c)**. End with an MC two-drop.

❷ Work the next row in AC.

❸ Work an MC two-drop. Pick up a square bead **(photo d)** in place of a three-drop. Do another MC two-drop.

❹ Repeat step 2, sewing through the square **(photo e)**.

❺ Repeat step 1.

❻ From now on, work three main-color rows between the square-bead motifs.

❼ End the bracelet with four main-color rows.

ADD THE MAGNETIC CLASP

❶ To attach one half of the magnetic clasp, follow the stringing pattern shown in **figure 5, a–b**. Repeat the thread path connecting the clasp to the bracelet several times. Tie several half-hitch knots (see "Basics") and dot with glue. Weave in the tail. Repeat on the opposite end.

Two-needle peyote start

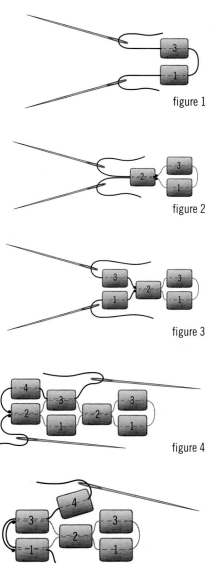

figure 1

How many times have you tried to start a peyote stitch project and found yourself with a tangled mess, vowing you'll never try to do peyote stitch again? If you're like most, it's happened more than once. Here's a handy two-needle technique that works great. This method builds the first three rows at once. You'll be thrilled at how easy it makes starting a peyote project—even in the middle.

Note: these directions are for peyote stitching from the bottom up. To peyote stitch from the top down, transpose row 1 and row 3 so that row 1 is on top.

❶ Thread two needles onto a single thread, one at each end.

❷ Pick up two beads: a row 1 bead on the bottom needle and a row 3 bead on the top needle. Slide them both to the center of the thread sitting side by side (**figure 1**).

❸ Pick up the next row 2 bead and pass both needles through it at the same time in the same direction. Pull the bead next to the first two beads (**figure 2**).

❹ Pick up two beads, the next row 3 bead on the top needle and the row 1 bead on the bottom needle, and pull them next to the single bead with #3 above #1. You may need to persuade the beads to sit properly by holding both threads and gently pushing them toward the single bead (**figure 3**). Keep an even tension.

❺ Repeat steps 3 and 4 until the piece is as wide as needed.

❻ For even-count flat peyote: End with a single bead as in **figure 2**. Drop the bottom needle and use the top one as the working thread to begin row 4 (**figure 4**).

❼ For odd count flat peyote: End with two beads as in **figure 3**. Pass the needle from row 3 into the last bead of row 1, heading back toward the work.

Tie this thread off or use it later. Pass the needle from row 1 into the last bead of row 3, heading back toward the work and use it to begin row 4 (**figure 5**).

❽ For even-count tubular peyote: Build the first three rows as for even-count flat peyote. Make a tube by bringing the beginning beads around to meet the last bead added. Make sure the strip isn't twisted. Then pass the bottom needle through the first bead in row 1 and the top needle through the first bead in row 3. Knot the bottom thread around the thread between beads #1 and #2. Use the top needle as the working thread to begin row 4 (**figure 6**).

❾ For odd-count tubular peyote: Build the first three rows as for odd-count flat peyote. Join into a tube as above, but pass both needles through the first bead in row 3. Knot the bottom thread around the thread between beads #3 and #2. Use the top needle to begin row 4 (**figure 7**).

– *Barbara L. Grainger*

figure 2

figure 3

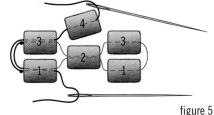

figure 4

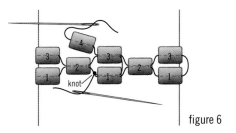

figure 5

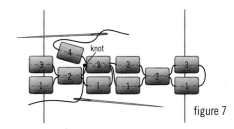

figure 6

figure 7

Snake trail bracelet

This bracelet gets its serpentine waves by contrasting the round shape of a seed bead with a slightly larger square-shaped bead in this simple even-count flat peyote-stitch pattern. The square profile of the beads in the triangle insets forces the round seed beads to curve to accommodate them, giving the bracelet its undulating shape.

Use beads of various sizes to make these bracelets, but try to keep the bead choices no more than one or two sizes apart. For the green and gold bracelet at lower left, size 10º seed beads are paired with size 8º hex-cut beads. The pink and burgundy bracelet is made with size 11º seed beads and size 10º twisted hex beads. The burgundy bracelet is made with size 11º seed beads and size 10º triangle beads. The large-scale silver cuff is made with size 6º seed beads and size 5º cube beads.

1 Thread a needle with 2 yd. (1.8m) of conditioned Nymo B doubled. Doubling the thread fills the bead holes and makes it easier to keep the tension taut so the smaller beads will curve around the larger beads.

2 Following the pattern below, begin an even-count, flat peyote piece (see "Basics," p. 5). *Note: the pattern is sideways. Beginning in the upper left-hand corner, string 12 small-sized beads for rows 1 and 2.* Use the large beads for the triangular insets and the small beads for the background. Keep the tension snug as you stitch.

3 Stitch the triangle repeat until the bracelet fits comfortably around your wrist. This will vary according to the bead sizes you choose.

4 To make a clasp, choose a coordinating button or large bead and sew it to the center of one end of the bracelet. (Alternatively, you can use two smaller buttons, spacing them evenly at the end of the bracelet.)

MATERIALS
- 10g seed beads
- 10g hex-cut, cube, or triangle beads (one or two bead sizes larger than the seed beads)
- 1 or 2 buttons or large beads for clasp
- Nymo B beading thread
- beeswax
- beading needles, #10 or 12

Reinforce the button attachment by sewing through it several times. Zigzag through the beads to end your thread and trim.

5 To make a loop for the button, start a new thread at the other end of the bracelet, zigzagging through the beads to secure the end. Exit the last bead on the bracelet's edge. String an even number of beads to create a loop large enough to go around the button snugly. (If you use two buttons, make two loops by sewing through the central "up" bead on the end of the bracelet.)

6 Sew through the end bead on the other edge of the bracelet, turn and begin to peyote stitch back along the loop's beads **(photo)**.

7 Add another row of peyote stitch for a total of four rows. (The beads strung for the loop are the first two rows.) Stitch back into the beadwork, zigzagging to secure the thread before trimming it. – *Kay A. Hutchison*

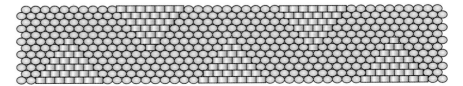

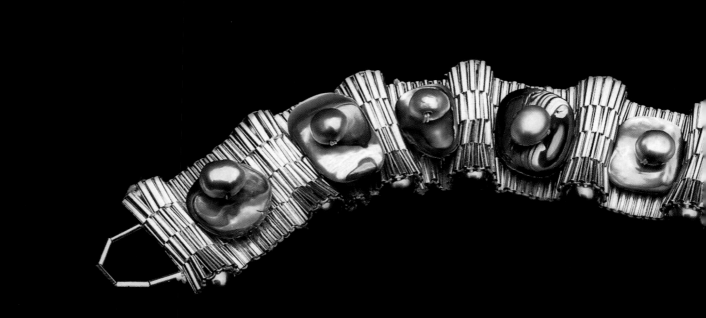

Silver sensation bracelet

Color, form, and texture are the elements of good design, and it's important to incorporate these concepts into your beading.

This bracelet combines the soft colors of abalone with the shine and surface detail of thin silver tubes in peyote stitch. The silver tubes are stitched into cylinders that divide the bracelet into sections. Pearls enhance the bracelet's texture and shape.

If you wish, try this design in gold and with bugle beads. Instead of putting pearls in the tubes, try rod-shaped beads for support. You can also try fanciful buttons and beads in place of the abalone.

❶ String four silver tube beads on 5 ft. (1.5m) of beading thread. Work in flat peyote (see "Basics," p. 5) for 24 rows (12 beads on each edge).

❷ Zip up the first and last rows of peyote to form a tube (see "Basics" and photo a). Go back through the beads to reinforce the connection.

❸ To make the clasp loop, sew through the beads until you are on the side of the tube opposite the join. Exit the second bead from the edge with your needle pointing toward the edge. String five or more beads (the loop must be large enough to fit over a piece of abalone) and go through the second bead from the opposite edge, exiting at the center (photo b). Go through these beads again to reinforce the loop.

❹ Weave through the beads and exit through any bead along the edge. String a 6mm pearl and insert the needle through the center of the peyote tube (photo c). Tighten the thread to lodge the pearl in the tube's opening. Make a small half-hitch knot (see "Basics")

around the thread between any of the beads at the opposite edge from the pearl. String another pearl, go back through the tube, and make a half-hitch knot to secure this pearl, as before. Dab the knots with glue.

❺ Weave through the beads along the edge row and exit a bead on the side of the tube opposite the loop. Work in flat peyote stitch for 18 rows (nine beads on each edge). If your abalone nugget or other accent bead is larger than 12 or 13mm wide, add rows of flat peyote as necessary, but you may have to adjust the total number of tubes and flat sections to maintain the bracelet's overall length.

❻ Maneuver back through the flat peyote panel and exit any bead at its center. String the abalone nugget and a flat pearl and go back through the nugget and peyote panel (photo d).

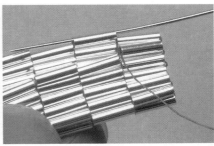

a

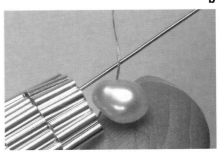

b

c

d

Tighten the thread so the beads sit against the band. Go up through these beads and back down again. Weave back through the peyote section and exit at either edge of the end row.

7 Continue making peyote tubes and flat sections until the bracelet is the desired length. Use the last abalone and pearl embellishment for your clasp.

– *Kelly Nicodemus-Miller*

MATERIALS

- **800** sterling tube beads, 5 x 1.5mm (available from Rio Grande, www.riogrande.com, 800-545-6566)
- **18** 6mm round pearls
- **9** button-shaped (flat-bottom) side-drilled pearls
- **9** abalone nuggets (available from Shipwreck Beads, 800-950-4232) or other center-drilled accent beads, approx. 12 x 15mm
- Power Pro beading cord or Fireline fishing line, 6-lb. test
- beading needles, #10
- G-S Hypo Cement or clear nail polish

Peyote-framed pearl bracelet

Frame a mabé pearl with a peyote-stitch bead bezel, embellish it with pearls, and then attach it to a band of five-drop peyote. Sew on a snap to use as your bracelet's clasp.

MABÉ PEARL BEZEL

1 Apply a thin, even layer of cement to the back of the mabé pearl and glue the pearl to the Ultrasuede. Set it aside to dry.

2 Trim the Ultrasuede, leaving approximately ⅛ in. (3mm) around the pearl's edge. Stitch through the Ultrasuede several times to anchor your thread. With the Ultrasuede facing you, pick up a bead and stitch through the fabric so the bead is parallel to and about ¹⁄₁₆ in. (2mm) from the edge **(photo a)**. Go through the bead again.

3 Continue with two-bead backstitch (see "Basics," p. 5) to sew beads around the edge of the Ultrasuede until you're back at the starting point **(photo b)**. Go through a few beads along this base row. (This counts as rows 1 and 2.)

4 Work in peyote stitch (see "Basics," p. 5) around the base row until you're back at the start. (This is row 3.)

5 If the bead count for row 3 is even, step up to start the next row (see "Basics"). If the count is odd, continue

without the step-up. As you stitch row 4, decrease (see "Basics") three or four beads equally spaced around the pearl.

6 Step up (even count) or simply continue (odd count) stitching to start the fifth and final row. As you stitch, place two beads in each decrease made in the previous row.

7 Determine where you want to place the teardrop pearl embellishment. Sew through the beads in row 5 until you reach your desired starting point and exit an "up" bead along the last peyote row. Pick up two beads, a teardrop pearl, and two beads. Stitch into the next "up" bead **(photo c)**. Repeat until you've embellished approximately half the mabé pearl's perimeter.

8 Turn and continue the embellishment along row 3. Secure the thread in the beadwork.

BAND

1 Work with a long strand of thread, waxed and doubled, but don't knot the tails.

2 Deduct 1 in. (2.5cm) from your wrist measurement. Pick up the amount of beads to equal this length, then add or remove beads until the count is a multiple of 10. (You can adjust the finished length slightly

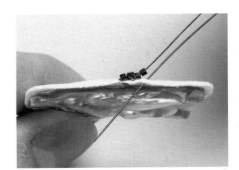

a

b

c

g

d

h

e

f

when you assemble the bracelet and attach the snaps.) Slide the beads to about 6 in. (15cm) from the tail ends.

❸ Work in five-drop peyote, as follows: pick up five beads, skip five beads, and go through the next five beads (figure). Repeat across the row.

❹ Continue until you have a total of 13 rows. The band will be just under ½-in. (1.3cm) wide. Stitch additional rows if you prefer a wider band, ending with an odd number of rows.

❺ With your thread exiting a "down" set of beads at the end of the last row, pick up two beads, a pearl, and two beads and stitch through the five high beads in the neighboring set (photo d). Continue making pearl picots across the row.

❻ When you reach the end of the first side, zigzag through to the other side of the bracelet. Repeat step 5, adding pearl picots on the other edge of the band. Secure the thread in the beadwork.

ASSEMBLY

❶ Start a new thread and exit a corner bead at the band's edge just below a pearl picot.

❷ Pick up a bead and go through the five-bead drop below the top corner (photo e). Turn and go back to the edge through the five-bead group below it. Repeat twice, adding a total of three beads along the band's short edge.

❸ Peyote stitch across the newly added beads (photo f). If you need to increase the band's length, add a few more peyote rows. Go through these beads again several times to reinforce them.

❹ Stitch the band to a few beads on the unembellished section of the mabé pearl (photo g). Go through these beads several times to reinforce the stitches and secure the thread in the beadwork.

CLASP

❶ Stitch half the snap onto the end of the bracelet band (photo h, left).

❷ Before you stitch the other snap half onto the Ultrasuede, check the fit again. Position the snap for the most comfortable fit, then sew it into place (photo h, right). Glue all the knots and trim any thread tails.

– Janet Flynn

MATERIALS— NARROW BRACELETS

- Mabé pearl approx. 1¼ in. (3cm) diameter
- 10g Japanese cylinder beads
- **38–44 teardrop pearls**
- Ultrasuede
- Nymo D beading thread
- beeswax or Thread Heaven
- beading needles, #10
- medium-sized metal snap
- barge cement or E6000 glue

Peyote window bracelet

Peyote stitch is a favorite among many beaders. It's versatile and creates an attractive woven appearance. This bracelet maintains the smooth look of flat peyote, but has added depth and the look of a fabricated piece of jewelry. Build the peyote-window bead in three stages: Work a peyote piece ten beads wide by ten rows to create the first tube. Build the second tube as an extension of the first by working a two-bead by ten-row strip at each end of tube #1. Finally, make the third tube full-size and attach it to the second tube at each end. This bracelet uses five window beads and is 7 in. (18cm) long, including the clasp. You will need five to seven window beads, depending on how long you want to make your bracelet.

MAKE THE WINDOW BEAD

1 Thread a needle with 24 in. (61cm) of Nymo. String a cylinder bead and go through it again in the same direction, leaving a 4-in. (10cm) tail.

2 String nine more beads and work even-count flat peyote (see "Basics," p. 5) for a total of ten rows (counting diagonally) (photo a).

3 After you complete the last row, remove the extra thread loop on the first bead and weave in the tail. Roll the piece into a tube and stitch through the high beads, alternating between the first and last rows (photo b). Zigzag back through the joining row again.

4 Create tube #2 as an extension of the first tube (see figure). Come out through a bead at the right-hand end of the tube (figure, point a), pick up a bead (photo c), and sew through the bead at point b on tube #1, exiting at point c. Add another bead. Working in peyote, add a strip two beads wide by ten rows. When you've added the tenth bead, zigzag back down the strip from point d.

5 Roll the strip into a tube and zip it closed by zigzagging between the two beads on tube #1 where the strip began and the last two beads of the strip (photos d–f). End by exiting the last bead on the strip (photo f and point e).

6 Weave across the tube from point f to point g (photo g). Repeat steps 4 and 5 starting at point g (photo h).

a

d

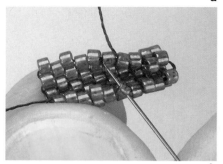

b

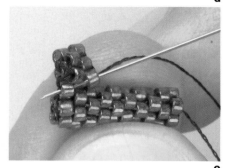

e

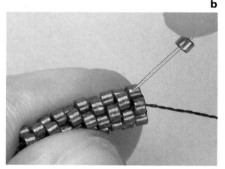

c

f

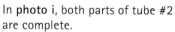

In **photo i**, both parts of tube #2 are complete.

7 Make tube #3 by repeating steps 1 through 3.

8 Zip tube #3 to tube #2 (photo j) to form a peyote-window bead.

STRING THE BRACELET

1 Determine the finished length of the bracelet, add 4 in. (10cm), and cut three pieces of flexible beading wire to that length. Attach one end of each wire to the clasp using a crimp bead for each (see "Basics").

2 On each strand, string a 2mm silver bead, a 4mm fire-polished bead, a flat spacer, a fire-polished bead, a flat spacer, a fire-polished bead, and a flat spacer, covering both the wire and its tail (photo k).

3 Pass the two outer wires through the outer tubes on a window bead. String the middle wire through the first part of the center tube. Inside the window, string a 15° silver seed bead,

a flat spacer, a fire-polished bead, a flat spacer, and a 15° seed. Pass the wire through the second part of the tube (photo l). (Note: the 15° seed beads were omitted in our photo.)

4 String a flat spacer, a fire-polished bead, a flat spacer, a fire-polished bead, and a flat spacer.

5 Repeat steps 3-4 for the length of the bracelet. After the last window bead, string the starting group in reverse. Thread a crimp bead, then go through the loop on the other clasp part. Go back through the crimp and several beads, snug up the beads, and crimp the crimp bead.

– Rae Ann Wojahn

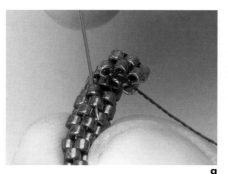

g

j

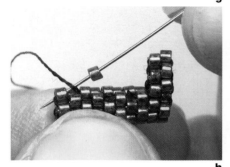

h

k

i

l

MATERIALS

- 5g size 11º Japanese cylinder beads
- **47–59** 4mm Czech fire-polished crystals
- **64–86** 4mm flat sterling silver daisy spacer beads
- **6** 2mm sterling silver spacer beads
- **10–14** size 15º seed beads, silver
- flexible beading wire, .012–.019
- Nymo B beading thread
- beeswax or Thread Heaven
- beading needles, #10 or 12
- toggle clasp
- **6** crimp beads

Tools: crimping or chainnose pliers, wire cutters

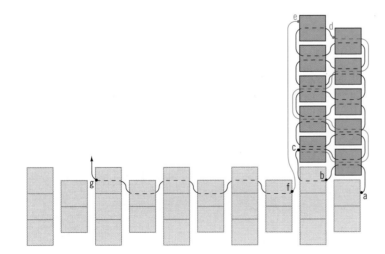

Bejeweled

peyote bracelet

Begin the bracelet by making a peyote-stitch platform for each cabochon. Set each stone onto its platform with beadwork. Next, assemble the bracelet with the spacer bars. This bracelet is 7 in. (18cm) long end to end, and the center platform is slightly larger than the side platforms, which improves the fit. For a small bracelet, 6-6½ in. (15-16.5cm), you might choose narrower spacer bars or set the two end cabochons vertically on narrower peyote platforms.

MAKING A PEYOTE-STITCH PLATFORM

① Thread a needle with 4 yd. (3.7m) of doubled, waxed Nymo B. String an 11º seed bead, slide it about 8 in. (20cm) from the end, and tie an overhand knot around it. This is the stop bead, which will prevent the other beads from falling off. Remove it later and weave in the tail.

② Pick up an even number of hex-cut beads (here, 14) and slide them to the stop bead.

③ Pick up a hex bead (#15) and pass the needle back through #13, skipping bead #14 (see "Basics," p. 5 for even-count flat peyote stitch). Continue peyote stitching to the end of the row **(photo a)**.

④ To start the next row, pick up a bead and pass the needle back through the last bead added. Pick up a bead and pass the needle through the next high bead. Continue peyote stitching in this manner until you've completed an even number of rows (22-26) and the piece is at least four rows wider than the cabochon.

SETTING A CABOCHON

① Center the stone on top of the peyote-stitch platform. While holding it in place, stitch through the beadwork to one side of the stone **(photo b)**.

② Pick up as many 11º seed beads as it takes to go around the stone; make this an even number. Go through the first 11º bead again to form a loop and pull the thread tight so the loop fits the stone snugly.

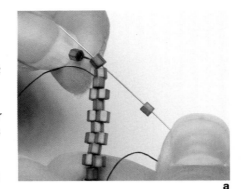

a

c

b

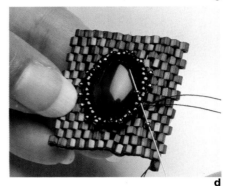

d

③ Hold the stone in place as you attach the bead loop around it to the platform as follows: Pass the needle through the closest hex bead in the platform and then through two beads in the loop **(photo c)**. Skip one or two hex beads and go through the next hex bead. Skip one or two seed beads on the loop and go through the next one or two seed beads. (Note: the curve of the cabochon will dictate how many beads you skip and which beads you go through. At the ends of the stone, where the edges are parallel to the holes of the hex beads, you'll have to go around the thread between hex beads.)

④ Go through all the loop beads again and pull the thread tight.

⑤ Unless your stone is thick and hasn't begun to round yet, begin the second row of the bezel with 14-15º seed beads and work in circular even-count peyote stitch (see "Basics"). (If the stone is thick, you may need one more row of 11ºs.) Pick up a bead, skip a bead on the loop, and pass your needle through the next bead on the loop. Repeat around.

⑥ When you get back to where you began, work the "step-up" by going

through the next bead on the first row of the loop and then the first bead added in this row **(photo d)**. For thin stones, one more row of peyote stitch will be enough. Finish by passing the needle through all the beads of the last row and pulling the thread tight **(photo e)**.

⑦ Stitch through the bezel and into the platform.

⑧ Embellishment: Surround the bezel with stone chips, each secured with a 14-15º bead **(photo f)**. You might also work a row of 11º seed beads between the beads of the first and last rows on the platform. If desired, work the corner trim shown in **photo j** now: Sew three 14-15º beads between the two corner beads on all four corners of each platform.

⑨ Make two more platforms, set the other two cabochons, and embellish. Make the center platform larger than the others, if desired, by beginning with 16 hex beads, rather than 14.

CONNECTING THE PLATFORMS

① Lay the three platforms on your work surface with two spacer bars between them. Center the pieces and

e

g

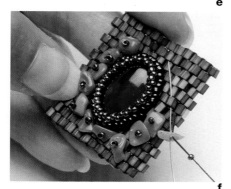

f

h

i

j

note where the holes on the spacer bars align with the hex beads.

❷ Bring the needle on the first platform out the hex bead that aligns with the top hole on the spacer bar. Pick up a hex bead, go through the hole on the bar, pick up another hex bead, and go into the same hex bead on the second platform (photo g).

❸ Weave the needle back and forth in the second platform so you can go back out the same hex bead you entered. Go through the beads and spacer bar and into the bead from which you began on the first platform (photo h).

❹ Weave over on the first platform and exit the hex bead that aligns with the center hole of the bar. Pick up a hex bead, go through the bar, pick up another hex bead, and enter the appropriate hex bead on the second platform. Repeat step 3.

❺ Repeat step 4 going through the bottom hole on the bar. If you have at least 18 in. (46cm) of thread left, do not end it. If a short length remains, end it and begin a new one.

❻ Repeat steps 2–5 to connect the second spacer bar and the third platform to the second platform.

MAKING THE BUTTON LOOP

❶ Go back to platform #1 and weave around the platform to exit the hex bead on the other edge that aligns with the bottom hole on the third spacer bar. Pick up a hex bead, go through the hole on the bar, and string enough 11º seed beads to make a loop that fits over the button.

❷ Sew through the top hole of the spacer bar, pick up a hex bead, and enter the appropriate hex bead on the platform (photo i). Weave the needle back and forth to exit the same hex bead and go back through the spacer bar and loop to reinforce them.

❸ Weave the needle through the platform to exit the hex bead that aligns with the center hole on the bar. Pick up a hex bead, go through the center hole, string a stop bead (an 11º or a 14º). Skip the stop bead and go back through the hole. Weave the needle into the platform to secure the thread before cutting it.

ATTACHING THE BUTTON

❶ Make a small peyote-stitch platform with hex beads. This platform needs to be long enough to attach a spacer

MATERIALS

- size 8º hex-cut seed beads (twisted or plain)
- size 11º and 14–15º seed beads, one or two colors in each size
- 4 three-hole spacer bars, approx. ¾–1 x ⅜ in. (2–2.5cm x 1cm)
- 3 cabochons, 18 x 13mm
- 45–50 small stone chips
- Nymo B beading thread
- beeswax or Thread Heaven
- beading needles, #12
- shank button

bar but just a few beads wide (here, six) so you can sew a button onto it.

❷ Connect the small platform and the fourth spacer bar as described in "connecting the platforms."

❸ Weave over the small platform to the place where you want the button. Then sew through the button shank and hex beads several times to secure it (photo j). If desired, add three-bead trim between pairs of beads along the edge of the button platform. Weave the thread securely into the platform before cutting it. – *Cheri Lynn Waltz*

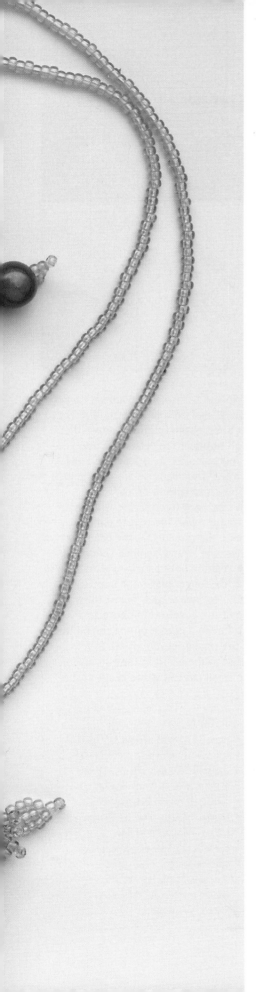

Wood rose necklace

Beaded flowers are a great way to affirm your love of gardening *and* beading, and they're exquisite when made with size 15º seed beads. Some people think size 15ºs are far too small to work with, though, so I adapted my technique to size 11º beads. Attach your floral creations to a "field of green" necklace and plant a grassy garden of flowers around them.

MAKE THE WOOD ROSE

❶ Thread a needle with 7 ft. (2.1m) of Nymo. String 20 flower-color seed beads, leaving a 1-yd. (.9m) tail. Tie the working thread and tail together in a firm square knot (see "Basics," p. 5) around a dowel. Sew through the first bead strung again.

❷ Stitch three rows of even-count, circular peyote (see "Basics") for a total of five rows. (The first two rows are the beads strung in step 1.) Step up on the fifth row as if you were going to add another row.

❸ Pick up three beads and stitch through the next bead in the fifth row of peyote again (photo a). Repeat to add three-bead "petals" between each bead in the fifth row for a total of ten petals.

❹ Stitch into the exterior surface of the previous (fourth) peyote row. Add five-bead petals between each bead in this row.

❺ Remove the beadwork from the dowel. Stitch into a nearby bead in the third row of peyote, exiting with your needle inside the sleeve. String an 8mm bead and sew through a third-row bead opposite the bead exited to anchor the 8mm bead in the sleeve (photo b). Sew back through the 8mm bead and the seed bead on the opposite side again. Repeat to secure the 8mm bead.

❻ Sew through another bead on the third row, exiting on the outside of the sleeve. Stitch seven-bead petals between the beads in this row (photo c). Sew through the beads in the next two peyote rows to secure the thread. Don't cut this tail. It will be used later to secure the flower to the base.

a

b

c

d

MAKE THE BASE

Use Fireline for the base and necklace strands for extra durability.

❶ Thread a needle with 7 ft. of Nymo or Fireline. String six green seed beads, leaving a 4½-ft. (1.3m) tail.

❷ Turn and stitch a panel of even-count flat peyote (see "Basics") with 30 rows. Don't trim the tail.

❸ Repeat step 1. Stitch a second flat, even-count peyote panel with 20 rows.

❹ Thread a needle on the 4½-ft. tail of the large peyote panel. String 8-9 in. (20-23cm) of green seed beads (photo d). Repeat with the small peyote panel.

❺ End the strands with either a large bead and loop closure or bead tips and a clasp as described below:

To make a bead and loop closure, string a 6mm bead, an 8mm bead, and four seed beads on one strand. Skip three seed beads and sew back through a seed bead and the large beads. Tighten so the three seed beads form a picot. To make a loop on the second strand, string a 6mm, an 8mm, and enough seed beads for a loop large enough to go over the 8mm bead. String three extra seed beads. Sew back through the first three seed beads and the larger beads to make the loop. Tie a few half-hitch knots between beads on the strand and sew back into the peyote panel. Repeat the thread path for security.

To use a clasp, string a bead tip and a seed bead, sew back through the bead tip, and tighten (photo e). Close the bead tips over the beads and use roundnose pliers to gently curve the hooks of the bead tips around the loop of the clasp (photo f).

❻ Sew back through the strand and zigzag through the peyote panel to secure the thread. Exit the bead next to where the strand is joined (photo g).

❼ Position both panels in a V-shape so that the longer one is the point and both necklace strands are at the inside top of the panels as in photo h.

❽ Thread a needle on the thread tail of the smaller peyote panel. Stitch between the beads in the end row of the small panel and the beads at the

MATERIALS
- 8mm round bead or pearl
- 15g size 11º seed beads, green
- 10g size 11º seed beads, floral color
- assorted 4-6mm flower beads
- ⅜-in. (1cm) diameter dowel
- Nymo D beading thread or Fireline fishing line, 4- or 6-lb. test
- beeswax or Thread Heaven for Nymo
- beading needles, #13
- clasp and 2 bead tips or 2 6mm and 2 8mm round beads for loop clasp

Tools: roundnose pliers

e

g

i

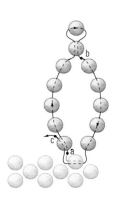

f

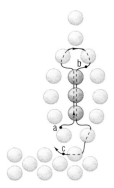

h

j

edge of the large panel to join them **(photo h)**. Zigzag through the peyote panel to secure the thread.

EMBELLISH THE PANEL

❶ Begin embellishing the panel ends with leaf shapes. Use the thread tails remaining from stringing each necklace strand and stitch a leaf as follows:

a. Pick up seven beads. Skip the last bead strung and go back through the next bead **(figure 1, a–b)**.

b. Pick up five beads and sew through the last bead exited on the base and the first bead strung **(figure 1, b–c)**.

c. Pick up three beads and sew up the fifth bead on the left side and through the fifth bead on the right side **(figure 2, a–b)**.

d. Sew back through the three beads just added and through the first bead on the right side of the leaf and the base bead **(figure 2, b–c)**.

❷ Add a leaf to each bead on the end rows of each panel. Zigzag through the panel to secure the thread and trim.

❸ Thread a needle to a remaining tail where the panels are joined or start a new thread at the panel's point. Stitch a leaf at the point and on each side of it **(photo i)**.

❹ Thread a needle onto the 3-ft. tail on the wood rose. Position the flower at the center of the V-shaped panel and stitch it in place **(photo j)**.

❺ Stitch two leaves to each side of the flower.

❻ Add flower bead and seed bead fringes to the sides of the panel. String a few seed beads, a flower bead, and another seed bead. Skip the last bead and sew back through the beads to the panel. Make some grassy fringes, too, without flower beads. Continue to embellish the panel until you are satisfied. – *Diane Benton*

figure 1

figure 2

Captive cabochons

If you want to use a cabochon as a pendant but don't want to attach it to a backing, use this technique for making a backless bezeled cabochon. Make a ring of even-count peyote stitch that begins with a circle a little smaller (about 20percent) than the circumference of the back of the cabochon. As you work out around the ring, adjust the thread tension so the ring remains flat. When the beadwork placed beneath the cabochon extends a little beyond the edges of the stone, work tighter rows until the frame overlaps the top of the stone enough to hold it in place without glue.

❶ Thread a needle with about 2 yd. (1.8m) of Nymo B. Double the thread and wax it. Pick up 60 size 11º seed beads. *Note: Select small beads for this first row.* Tie the ends together with a square knot (see "Basics," p. 5), forming a tight circle and leaving a 6-in. (15cm) tail. Tension is critical in this project, and the circle should be the tightest row of all **(photo a)**.

❷ Go through the first bead after the knot and work peyote stitch around the circle (see "Basics"). The tension should now be snug but not tight. Hold the beads between your fingers as you tighten them to help keep the work flat and to prevent overtightening **(photo b)**.

❸ On every successive row, the tension will be a little looser in order to keep the work flat. After every row, shape the piece against the bottom of the cab and check the size. The last row, here the seventh, will extend at least half a bead beyond the edge of the cab **(photo c)**. When using two colors, you may want to work the last row in the second color to give a visual reference.

❹ After completing the last row, weave the thread back into the beadwork to anchor it securely. Make two or three half-hitch knots (see "Basics") between beads as you weave in the thread.

❺ Start a new 2-yd. doubled, waxed thread, weaving it securely into the piece. Come out a bead on the last row. From this point on, you'll pull and tighten the thread after every bead, so now is a good time to take a break and do a few hand and wrist exercises. Once you start shaping,

a

b

c

it's hard to stop until you're finished.

❻ Hold the cabochon on top of the piece so you can form the beadwork around its sides. Don't put too much tension on the outside until you've added two more rows and the beadwork is coming up the sides **(photo d)**.

❼ As you bead around the edge of the cab, keep the tension as tight as possible. When you near the upper edge, select smaller beads to help bring the beading in over the top **(photo e)**. You'll be able to tell by feel when you have completed enough rows to hold the stone securely. Fewer rows are better, but make sure you have enough rows to hold the cab. Because of shape, thickness, curvature, and polish, each stone requires a different number of rows for security.

❽ After completing the last row, go back through it again, following the

d

e

f

peyote stitch pattern **(photo f)**. This second thread pass is important to help maintain the tension on the cab, so tighten it carefully as you go to keep it from breaking. Weave the thread into the beadwork away from the edge to secure it. Then trim.

Highlight your cabochon in a necklace, as pictured on the opposite page. I worked my bezeled stone into a rope of Dutch spiral, which I learned from Anna Maria Garcia. – *Elisa Cossey*

MATERIALS

- 30 x 40mm oval cabochon (stone or glass)
- size 11º Czech seed beads in one or two colors (for bezel only)
- Nymo beading thread, size B, or Silamide
- beeswax for Nymo
- beading needles, #12 or 13

Ruffled brooch

In 1995, Wendy Ellsworth experienced a creative breakthrough with her SeaForm Series of undulating, intensely ruffled peyote stitch organic vessels (see p. 89 for vessel instructions). "I began setting a variety of different cabochons in the center of my SeaForm vessels by beading a gourd stitch bezel to hold them in place and then surrounding them with a wild ruffle. Soon I realized that with the same idea, I could create a snappy little pin or pendant, a miniature SeaForm that was both affordable and much quicker to make," she says.

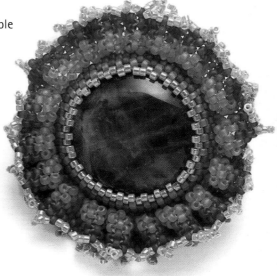

HELPFUL HINTS

• Put beeswax on the end of Silamide bead thread to make threading easier.
• Keep tension even and tight.
• Watch out for the thread hooking itself around another bead as you stitch.
• When doing radical increases in the ruffle, cull through the beads to find two thin beads for the two-bead increase. On the next row, use a thin bead between each two-bead increase. This leaves less of a gap, which makes the increases less noticeable.
• Don't use black or cut beads when you first try this project. They're hard to see.
• The size variation of Czech seed beads works well for radical increasing. The effect will be different with Japanese cylinder beads.
• Thread color should match bead color. Choose the largest size that will fit through your beads three times.
• Use "sharps" needles to sew through leather. Long beading needles tend to bend and break too easily.

First mount the cabochon on leather, Ultrasuede, or Stiff-Stuff. Start the bezel with a row of backstitch and complete it with several rows of peyote stitch. Next install the pin back. Then work about 12 rows of peyote stitch with radical increases. Finish with a simple edging.

PREPARE THE CABOCHON

❶ Place the cabochon on a small piece of leather or other backing. Mark around the cabochon with a pen, following its contour. (Note: If the cabochon is small, cut the leather backing large enough to accommodate the length of the pin back.)
❷ Apply a multi-purpose cement to the back of the cabochon and the surface of the leather inside the pen line. Let the glue set up for 5-10 min. Then press the glued surfaces together. Cut out the leather around the cabochon about 1/8 in. (3mm) from the edge (photo a). Be careful to leave enough width to accommodate the width of the first row of beads. It's better to leave too much width that can be trimmed later.
❸ Place the cabochon on the wrong side of another piece of leather, trace

a

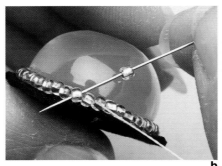

b

around it, and cut it out. Reserve this piece for the brooch's backing.

STITCH THE BEZEL

❶ Thread a "sharps" needle with about 1 yd. (.9m) of single thread. Tie two knots, one on top of the other, at one end. (If you prefer to work with doubled thread, you may do so after the first row.) I burn the tip of the thread to make a little ball beside the knot. If the ball sizzles up into the knot, start over.
❷ Pass the needle through the leather from back to front beside the cabochon. Work the first row in two-bead backstitch (see "Basics," p. 5).
❸ Continue around the base of the cabochon. When you get to the last stitch, you want to be able to fill the gap with two beads. If necessary, choose narrower or wider beads for the last few stitches so that two beads will fit. Take a normal back stitch but also continue through the first bead of the row. You are now ready to start the second row.
❹ Row 2 is the first row of peyote stitch (see "Basics"). Pick up a bead, skip the next bead on the base row, and go through the next bead (photo b). Continue around, adding a bead through every other bead on the base row. Keep the tension very tight and pull the new row of beads up onto the side of the cabochon.
❺ When you get to the end of the row,

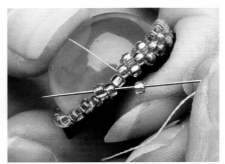

c

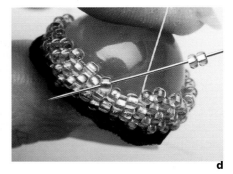

d

pass the needle through the first bead of the base row and the first bead of row 2. This puts you in position to begin row 3 (photo c).
❻ Depending on the size and shape of the cabochon, you'll either work plain peyote stitch for row 3, or you'll need to do an even number of evenly spaced decreases (see "Basics"). Sometimes just using thinner beads will accomplish the same thing as decreasing.
❼ Row 4 will probably require an even number of real decreases evenly spaced around the cabochon. To decrease, pass your needle through the next bead in sequence without adding a bead (see "Basics").
❽ Row 5 is the last row. Use a contrasting bead color or keep the color the same. Place one bead in each stitch. When you reach the places where you decreased in row 4, either add a very wide bead or two skinny ones to fill the gap (photo d). Go through all the beads of rows 4 and 5 again without adding beads to tighten and strengthen the edge of the bezel. Weave and tie your thread into the beadwork.

INSTALL THE PIN BACK

❶ Place the pin back above the mid-line on the right side of the second piece of leather. Mark both ends of the pin back on the leather and punch small holes or cut small slits there.
❷ Open the pin back and place the

radical increasing

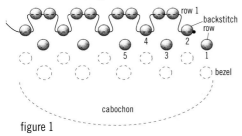

figure 1

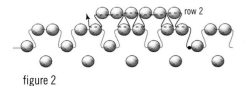

figure 2

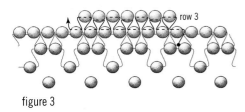

figure 3

edging

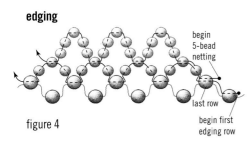

begin
5-bead
netting

last row

begin first
edging row

figure 4

e

f

g

wrong side of the leather over it. Push the pin through one hole and the catch through the other **(photo e)**. If you're using a pin back with a bail, punch a third hole where the bail connects to the pin back and slit the leather from the top edge down to this hole. Push the bail through the hole.

3 If necessary, trim the edge around the cabochon, being careful to not cut any threads. The ruffle covers some backing overlap. Apply cement to the back of the cabochon and the wrong side of the leather plus pin back.

4 Let the glue set up for 5-10 min. Then press the two pieces together.

MAKE THE RUFFLE

For your first brooch, use a different color bead for each of the first three rows. This helps you see where the beads are in the previous row so you'll

know where to take the next stitch. If the bead holes are large enough, use doubled thread.

1 Weave a new thread into the beadwork bezel so that it exits one of the "down" beads (closest to the backing) of the base row.

2 Row 1: String two beads and go through the next "down" bead. Repeat all the way around the base row **(figure 1)**. Pull after each stitch to keep the tension as tight as possible so that the next row doesn't get deformed. After adding the last two beads of the row, go through the first base-row bead again and the first bead added in the first stitch.

3 Row 2: The radical increase begins on this row. Add one bead, go through the next bead, add two beads, go through the next bead **(photo f)**. Repeat all the way around the row. Place each single-bead stitch in the middle of each two-bead stitch on row 1 **(figure 2)**. End this row by passing the needle through the first bead of row 1 and the first bead of row 2.

4 Row 3: To complete the radical increase, add one bead per stitch passing the needle through each bead of row 2. This is harder than it sounds. **Figure 3** makes the process look flat, but the beadwork undulates so much that it is often difficult to determine which is the next bead on row 2 **(photo g)**.

5 Rows 4-12: Continue to add one bead per stitch around every row. If you want to make the brooch ruffle more, add two beads per stitch wherever you choose in the row. On the subsequent row, put a bead between each two-bead increase, as on rows 2 and 3.

WORK AN EDGING

A simple edging technique is to add three beads per stitch around the whole last row. For a fuller effect, work a row of five-bead netting through the center bead of the three-bead increase **(figure 4)**. Use size 12º 3-cut Czech beads for the edging row(s) to add sparkle.
– *Wendy Ellsworth*

MATERIALS

- stone or glass cabochon (any size/shape)
- leather, Ultrasuede, or Stiff-Stuff for two backing pieces
- size 11º Czech seed beads, three or more colors, 1 hank or package per color
- hank or package size 12º 3-cut Czech seed beads (optional)
- Silamide or Nymo D or B beading thread to match main-color beads
- beeswax
- sharps needles, #12 or 11
- beading needles, #12 or 13, if desired
- pin back to fit cabochon
- barge cement or Bond 527

Cellini spiral
necklace

Circular peyote stitch takes on a sculptural look when it's worked in beads of various sizes. These sculptural spiral necklaces evolved from a technique taught by Virginia Blakelock and Carol Perrenoud at the Mid-Atlantic Fiber Arts Conference several years ago. Virginia developed the stitch and named it in honor of Benvenuto Cellini, a 16th-century Italian sculptor known for his rococo achitectural columns.

The Cellini spiral is essentially circular peyote executed with graduated beads. The tighter it's done, and the more contrast in the sizes of beads used, the more the work will pucker inward on the spiral of smaller beads.

Play with different color and size combinations before you begin. To get a better feel for how the finished necklace will look without making Cellini samples, make a bead ladder or work a two-bead strip of square stitch (see "Basics," p. 5).

The instructions below explain how to make the ivory and green necklace above, but you can adapt these

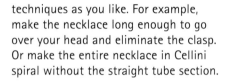

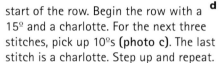

techniques as you like. For example, make the necklace long enough to go over your head and eliminate the clasp. Or make the entire necklace in Cellini spiral without the straight tube section.

1 Using a 1 yd. (.9m) or longer thread, begin work at the center of the necklace by making a straight tube as follows: String two 15ºs, four charlottes, two 15ºs, four charlottes. Tie the tail and working thread with a square knot to make a tight circle, leaving a 6-in. (15cm) tail. These beads comprise rows 1 and 2.

2 To begin row 3, take your needle through the first two 15ºs in the sequence (photo a). Pick up a 15º, go through the second charlotte, pick up a charlotte, go through the fourth charlotte, pick up a charlotte, go through the second 15º, pick up a 15º, go through the second charlotte, pick up a charlotte, go through the fourth charlotte, and pick up a charlotte. *(Note: Whether you're working the straight tube or the spiral, always pick up the same bead as the bead you've just gone through.)*

3 To step up for row 4, go through the second 15º on row 2 and the first on row 3. Pick up a 15º and go through the first row 3 charlotte (photo b). Continue in this pattern, stepping up for each new row until the tube measures 1 in. (2.5cm).

4 Now make two transition rows to the Cellini spiral. Step up as usual at the

start of the row. Begin the row with a 15º and a charlotte. For the next three stitches, pick up 10ºs (photo c). The last stitch is a charlotte. Step up and repeat.

5 Start the Cellini spiral by stepping up and substituting an 8º for the middle 10º. The Cellini sequence is 15º, charlotte, 10º, 8º, 10º, charlotte.

6 Keep the tension tight. After six to eight rows, the sculptural Cellini shape becomes well-defined (photo d). Continue working in Cellini spiral stitch for 3 in. (7.6cm).

7 To make the transition back to the straight tube, substitute a 10º for the 8º for two rows. To return to the original straight tube sequence, substitute a charlotte, a 15º, and a charlotte for the three 10ºs. Continue working the straight tube for ¾ in. (2cm).

8 Alternate between straight tube and Cellini spiral as desired, ending with the Cellini spiral, until you are about 2½ in. (6cm) from the finished length of one side of the necklace.

9 To taper the end of the necklace, work in the transition sequence (see step 7) for four rows. Now, reduce the number of beads from six to four as follows: Work the step up, then pick up a 15º, go through the charlotte, pick up a charlotte, go through the next charlotte and 15º, pick up a 15º, go through the next charlotte, pick up a charlotte, go through the next charlotte and 15º (photo e). Step up to start the next row. Work four-bead rows for 1½ in. (3.8cm).

10 Pick up two 15ºs and go back through the last charlotte and 15º added on the last peyote row (photo f).

11 Begin square stitch by going through the two 15ºs in the same direction as in step 10. Pick up two more 15ºs and work in two-bead square stitch for eight rows (see "Basics"). Slip the clasp finding on this strip and attach the strip securely to the other side of the spiral (photo g).

12 Weave in a new thread so it exits the starting point at the center of the necklace. Follow steps 4 to 11 to complete the second half. Weave in any loose threads. – *Deb Samuels*

g

MATERIALS

- 5-7g (approx.) seed beads in sizes 15º, 10º, 8º, and 13º charlottes
- Silamide or Nymo D beading thread
- beeswax or Thread Heaven for Nymo
- beading needles, #12
- clasp

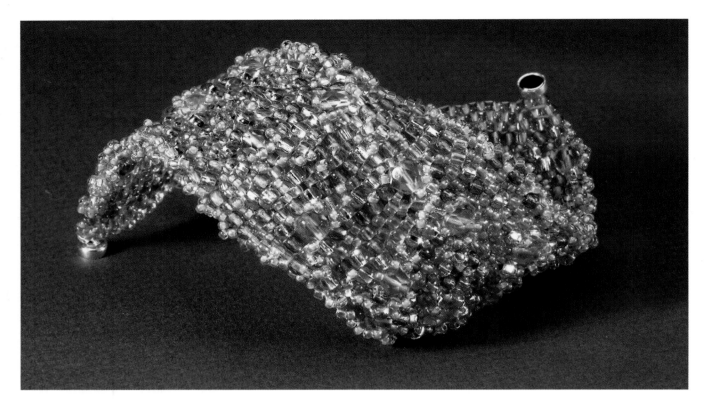

Free-form peyote bracelet

Adding a new technique to your repertoire is an exciting adventure. You never know where it will lead. In this case, an assortment of beads in various sizes and shapes dictate a random, free-form approach to peyote stitch to build the beads into a textured band. This bracelet is proof that you don't have to work on a new technique for ages before it becomes a useful tool. Even beginners can have fun and get great results.

Work the chunky bracelet lengthwise from a center spine of even-count flat peyote stitch. When the first half of the bracelet is about ¾ in. (2cm) wide, you work the other half out from the other edge of the spine.

The nubby texture is the result of using different sizes and shapes of beads. Begin by selecting five interestingly textured beads in the

approximate sizes and quantities listed in "materials." Most of the bracelet is made with the three smallest sizes; the two larger bead sizes are used randomly for accent. Work with long lengths of doubled, waxed thread, using a size that will pass through the smallest beads at least four times.

❶ Thread a needle with about 4 yd. (3.7m) of thread. Double and wax it. String a temporary stop bead to about 18 in. (46cm) from the end and go through the bead again to anchor it. Pick up enough beads to go around your wrist with the ends touching about 2 in. (5cm) above your wrist bone. String beads randomly for the base row, but do not use either the largest or the smallest beads. You need an even number of beads, excluding the stop bead.
❷ Work back across the base strand in

flat, even-count peyote stitch ("Basics," p. 5), picking up beads similar to the ones they touch (photo a). Check the band for length. If you need to add a few more beads, remove the stop bead and string the new beads onto the tail. Then peyote across them to the end of the row.
❸ Make sure the strip is not twisted and work back across the row, again picking up beads similar to the ones they touch. Work 2-3 more rows this way to establish a solid base for the experiments to come.
❹ When you have worked six rows (each stack is three beads high), you can begin adding a few large beads for texture. Look for shallow areas where a larger bead will fit comfortably. The thread should travel straight across with the large bead perhaps spanning two to four small beads (figure 1).

⑤ When you come to the large bead on the next row, use small or tiny beads before and after it to keep the work flat **(figure 2)**. When you return to the large bead on the third row, span it with two small beads even though three may fit **(figure 3)**. This allows room for large beads in subsequent rows. To eliminate a bulge in the following row, if necessary, you may want to pass through a bead or two without adding beads.

⑥ Robin's secret to getting smooth areas around her large beads is to work back and forth across small sections, rather than continuously across every row **(photo b)**. She works a smooth textural field back and forth across a few inches of the bracelet to build up several rows of "ledge" at the edge of which she places the large bead **(figure 4)**. Then she works the ledge across a few inches on the other side of the bead. To connect a new short section to an existing one, turn to work back by sewing through a ledge bead on the same level as the new row. Then reverse direction through the ledge bead above.

⑦ When the strip is ¾ in. wide, build up the center 3 in. (7.6cm) with a few more rows.

⑧ Finish off the outer edge by working small beads into any gaps. Don't worry about a few threads showing in the body of the work, you'll embellish over them later. If a long thread remains, leave it attached for finishing the ends and sewing on the clasps. Tape it under the bracelet to avoid tangling. If the thread is short, weave it in and clip the tail.

⑨ Attach a new thread to the base row and work the other side. Since you stabilized the spine in steps 1-3, you can begin adding large beads right away. Place large beads and design elements to balance the first side. When the bracelet is 1¼ in. (3cm) wide across the narrow edge, build up the center 3 in. as in step 7 and finish the edge as in step 8.

⑩ Now sew over to any places where threads show and embellish over them with small beads.

⑪ The ends are likely to be irregular. Bring a thread out the bead at one edge of an end and work a few rows of brick stitch across the edge to make a smooth finish **(photo c** and "Basics")**.

Check the bracelet for length, allowing for the clasp, and work a few more rows of brick stitch if needed.

⑫ If desired, overcast tiny beads along each long edge to finish them smoothly **(photo d)**.

⑬ Finally, sew the female halves of each clasp to the corners on one end of the bracelet and the male halves to the opposite corners.

– design by Robin Brisco; directions by Penny Harrell; bracelet beaded by Alice Korach. To see Robin's original bracelet made with chunky brass beads (which was, unfortunately, lost by the U.S. Postal Service) visit Robin's website, totheweb.com/robin/.

a

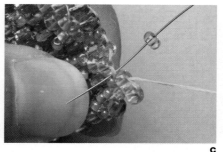

c

b

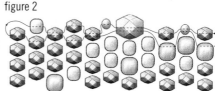

d

figure 1

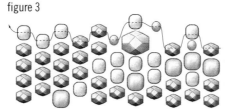

figure 2

figure 3

figure 4

MATERIALS
- 200+ 3mm fire-polished crystals
- 300+ size 8º seed beads
- 400+ size 11º seed beads
- 65+ size 6º seed beads
- 15+ 6mm pressed-glass crystals
- Nymo B or D or Silamide beading thread
- beeswax for Nymo
- beading needles, #12
- 2 box or magnetic clasps

Shaped necklace

Using a wire armature provides a flexible core support for beadwork and opens up a whole new realm of possibilities. I love to design with large focal beads and wire-wrapped pendants, but I found that even 20-gauge wire and peyote tubes with size 8° beads weren't substantial enough to successfully highlight the larger pieces. While rummaging around in the basement, I came across some electrical wire and knew I was on to something. Using even-count tubular peyote, I beaded a tube around the wire. Once the ends were closed, I created a focal bead dangle with a fringe tassel and formed the wire into a necklace that would hold its shape and still remain light and flexible enough to take on and off without a clasp. Success!

GETTING STARTED

If you are new to circular peyote, take a look at "Basics" on page 5. Many beaders prefer to do this stitch without anything inside the tube, but beading around the wire enables you to keep your stitches tight yet flexible enough to bend.

Electrical wire with black plastic coating is available at home improvement centers. Unlike metal wire, which is sized in gauges according to diameter, electrical wire is given an AWG number. I use #6AWG wire, which is stiff enough to hold its shape and happens to fit perfectly inside a peyote tube with this bead count.

Unless you already have bolt cutters at home, bring your measurements to the store and have them cut the wire for you. The necklace featuring a Kevin O'Grady bead (at left) is 21-in. (.53m) long without the dangle. The purple example on p. 52, with beads by Alethia Donathan, is 24-in. (.61m) long without dangles.

PEYOTE TUBE

❶ Thread a needle with 2 yd. (1.8m) of Fireline or Nymo. If you're using Nymo, double your thread and condition it with beeswax.

❷ Leaving a 10-in. (25cm) tail, string twelve beads in the following order: two color A (size 6°), two color B (size 8°), two color C (size 8°), two color A, two color B, and two color C.

❸ Tie these beads in a ring using a surgeon's knot (see "Basics"). Place the ring over the wire. Keep your thumb on the tail as you bead the first few rows so it doesn't get woven into the tube.

❹ Start at the knot, and working from right to left, go through the first A bead in the ring. Pick up one A and go through the first B. Pick up one B and go through the first C. Pick up one C and go through the first A (figure 1). Continue around until you come to the first A.

❺ To "step up" to the next row, go through the first A on the ring and the A you added in step 4. Pick up another A and go through the next B

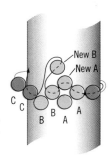

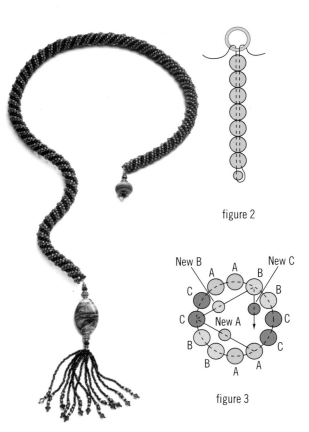

figure 2

New B   New C
New A

figure 3

a

b

ADDING THREAD
Don't wait until you are out of thread to add more. When you get down to your last 7 in. (18cm), go back through several beads, make a couple of half-hitch knots (see "Basics") and cut the thread. Rethread the needle with 2 yd. of new thread and tie a couple of half-hitches near the beads where you tied off. Go through several beads. Exit the same bead where you left off and continue from there.

(photo a). You'll notice the pattern starting to spiral. Keep your tension fairly tight, but not so tight that the tube won't bend. Continue until the tube reaches the end of the wire. Do not cut the thread yet.

MAKING THE DANGLE
❶ Cut a piece of 20-gauge wire 3-in. (7.6cm) longer than the combined length of your focal bead and spacers.
❷ Make a wrapped loop at one end (see "Basics").
❸ String accent beads and a focal bead as desired. Make a small wrapped loop at the top (photo b).
❹ You may wish to make a second, shorter dangle for the other end of the necklace.
❺ To make the fringe, thread a needle with 2 yd. of thread. Leaving a 7-in. (18cm) tail, tie an overhand knot (see "Basics") through the bottom loop of the dangle.
❻ String an assortment of beads and crystals to the desired tassle length.

❼ Go through the second-to-last bead strung and back through the rest of the beads until you exit at the top fringe bead (figure 2).
❽ Tie an overhand knot but do not cut the thread. Repeat steps 6 and 7, always tying a knot at the loop before beginning the next fringe.
❾ To finish, tie a final overhand knot through the loop and dot with glue. Go through several beads on the nearest fringe and cut the thread. Repeat with the tail.

FINISHING THE ENDS
❶ Starting with the step-up bead, pick up one A and go through the first C. Pick up one B and go through the next B. Pick up one C and go through the next A (figure 3). The tube will quickly close. You may need to add a bead in the center of the circle to fill the space. When the end is closed, make a half-hitch knot and go through several nearby beads, exiting at the center bead. Don't cut the thread.

❷ To attach the dangle, go through the top loop several times and back up through nearby beads. Tie a half-hitch knot and go back through the beads and the dangle loop again. Go through a few adjacent beads, tie a half-hitch knot, and dot with glue. Weave the tail back in and cut the thread.
❸ Repeat step 1 to finish the other end. If you are using a second dangle, repeat step 2 to attach it.
❹ Gently shape the necklace until it conforms to your neck and body. The shorter end should start just left of the center of your throat and curve around your neck. At the point slightly to the right of your throat, bend the piece in a right angle. – Mary Lou Allen

Russian leaves pendant or brooch

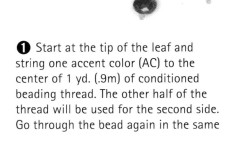

Russian leaves, done here in diagonal peyote stitch, have unlimited design possibilities. The leaves are beautiful on their own. When combined with other elements, they can be used to create stunning lariats, necklaces, bracelets, earrings, or brooches. Taking the versatility of the leaves one step further, I have designed a piece that can be worn as both a brooch and a pendant.

For this brooch, create each leaf individually and attach it to the surface of a flat piece of beadwork. Then attach a pin back, work a picot edge, and add branch fringe. Create a necklace by adding findings and a neck strap to the brooch.

Make the piece as lush as you like based on the number of leaves you add. Remember that an odd number is more appealing visually. I like to make the leaves in several colors, but you can make them all one color or use different shades of a color. These instructions are geared to making multi-color leaves. To make a single-color leaf, just omit the accent color.

MAKE A LEAF

Make the leaves one side at a time. Add veins to the center and work a picot edge around the outside. I worked the leaf with Japanese cylinder beads and the veins and edging with 14-15° seeds.

❶ Start at the tip of the leaf and string one accent color (AC) to the center of 1 yd. (.9m) of conditioned beading thread. The other half of the thread will be used for the second side. Go through the bead again in the same direction (you'll remove this extra pass before starting the second side).

❷ String five main color (MC), one AC, and one MC. Go through the fourth MC toward the start (photo a and figure 1, a–b). String one MC. Go

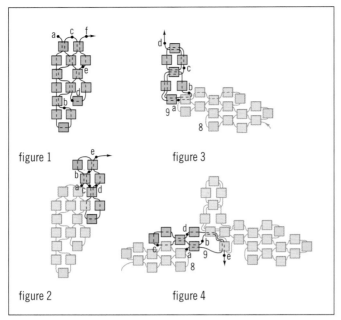

figure 1

figure 2

figure 3

figure 4

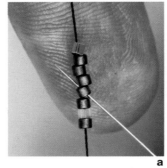

a

d

b

e

c

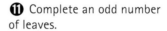

f

through the second MC. String one MC and go through the AC start bead (figure 1, b-c).

3 Turn and work two MC peyote stitches (figure 1, c-d). Then make a picot by stringing one AC and one MC. Turn the piece and go back through the last peyote stitch (figure 1, d-e). Work one MC peyote stitch (figure 1, e-f).

4 To begin the first and following diagonal peyote rows: String one MC, one AC, and one MC (figure 2, a-b). Go back through the first MC strung, pointing toward the tip (photo b and figure 2, b-c). The second MC will be next to the AC. Work one MC peyote stitch (photo c) then one picot (photo d and c-d). Finish the return row with one MC peyote stitch that goes through the second MC strung at the beginning of this step (photo e and d-e).

5 Repeat step 4 eight more times. There will be nine inside AC vein points plus the start AC bead (photo f).

6 To work the top stem, string 4 MC (figure 3, a-b). Go through the MC bead above the ninth AC vein bead

and through the first three of the four MCs to make a five-bead diamond (figure 3, b-c). Make a four-bead MC diamond above this bead with three more MCs (figure 3, c-d).

7 Go back to the starting tail and ease the extra thread loop out of the AC bead before you thread the needle. Repeat steps 3 and 4. Repeat step 5 seven more times for a total of eight inside vein points plus the start AC (photo g).

8 To connect the leaf sides, string one MC and go through the last AC on the first side from bottom-to-top. Continue through the first of the four beads strung in step 6 (figure 4, a-b).

9 Go through the MC bead added in step 8 and do one MC peyote stitch (figure 4, b-c) and one more picot on the second side of the leaf (figure 4, c-d).

10 Add one MC and go down through the first MC added in step 6 as well as the top center AC vein bead (figure 4, d-e). The needle now points into the center of the leaf to begin the veins.

11 Complete an odd number of leaves.

MAKE THE VEINS

Make the veins with 14-15º AC seeds or Japanese cylinder beads. Experiment with the number of beads you use for each vein and try skipping some of the vein-point beads. As no two leaves in nature are the exactly the same, these beaded leaves will each be different based on the way you make the veins.

1 String 25 beads in a loose vertical line, going into the center AC bead. (Note: figure 5 shows counts using cylinder beads.) Go through two MC beads on the left side of the inner edge as shown in figure 5, a-b. Exit the next vein bead (photo h). (Note: this photo shows

that you can go through more leaf-body beads than the figure shows, if you wish.)

2 For each vein, string from two to seven beads, connect through one to three beads on the central vein, and string the next vein, connecting to the leaf (figure 5). Work all veins as in figure 5 or vary them as you wish.

g

j

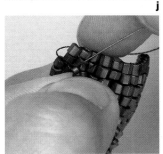

k

h

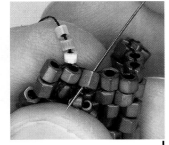

l

i

m

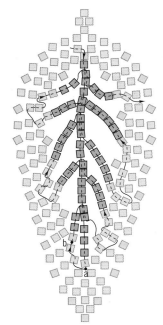

figure 5

EDGE THE LEAVES

The bead picots along the outside edge of the leaf give the leaf its natural, curvy shape. Work the edges with 14-15º seed beads.

❶ Position the needle so it comes out of an outside-edge AC at the very top of the leaf. Pick up three seeds beads. Bring the needle down through the next AC bead below it **(photo i)**. Continue picking up three beads and going down through the next AC bead until you reach the

tip of the leaf. Pull tightly to give the leaf its shape.

❷ Continue adding three beads along the other side of the leaf, this time going up through the AC beads.

❸ When you reach the stem of the leaf, work the thread through several beads, make two or three half-hitch knots (see "Basics," p. 5), and dab with glue to secure. Trim the thread close to the beads.

MAKE THE BASE

Create a beaded base where you will attach the leaves. For seven leaves, the number used in this brooch, you need a base that is approximately 1 x 1 in. (2.5cm). Adjust the size of the base according to the number of leaves you make. The base can be made with most seed beads, using the beading stitch of your choice. Here, 8º hex beads were used in two-drop peyote because it is fast and makes attaching the leaves easy. When you finish the base, you may want to go back through all the rows. This makes it sturdier and also makes attaching the leaves easier.

❶ Leaving a tail that you will weave in later, start with a 1-yd. (.9m) length of conditioned beading thread. String 12 size 8º seeds and begin two-drop peyote (see "Basics").

❷ Work subsequent rows in two-drop peyote until the piece measures 1 x 1 in. **(photo j)**. Zigzag back through the rows for added support. Weave in the tail,

work two or three half-hitch knots, and dab with glue to secure.

ATTACH THE LEAVES

Arrange the leaves on the base in a way that is aesthetically pleasing. Experiment before you attach them permanently. To orient the base correctly, the bead holes should run vertically along the top and bottom edges of the piece.

❶ Attach a 12-in. (30cm) length of conditioned beading thread to the base. Come out the middle bead in the top loop of the leaf. Tack the loop down to the base by weaving into a bead and back through the bead you exited on the loop **(photo k)**. Weave through the bead and loop again in the same direction. Don't weave in the thread until all the leaves are attached in this way.

❷ Attach all the leaves as described in step 1.

❸ Now position the leaves the way you want them to stay permanently and tack them down by zigzagging between a bead in a leaf and a bead in the base.

❹ Weave in the tails.

EDGE THE BASE

You may add a picot edge along the top of the brooch to create a more finished look. If the piece will be worn as a brooch and as pendant, don't picot the two top-edge corner beads on the base.

❶ Weave a new thread into the base and exit the second bead from the left top edge. Pick up three 11º beads. Go down through the bead to the right of the one you are exiting **(photo l)**. Pull tight to form the picot edge.

❷ Sew up out of the next bead. Pick up three seeds and

sew down into the fifth bead. Add three more picot sets (five sets total). Don't add a picot to the last bead.

3 Start a new thread and exit a corner 8º at the top edge of the base. String eight 14º seeds and go back through the 8º to form a loop. Weave into the base, then repeat the thread path several times to strengthen the loop. Repeat with the other corner bead on the top edge of the base.

FRINGE AND BRANCH FRINGE
Add fringe to every other bead across the bottom edge of the base. For a fuller look, work fringe from every bead.

1 Branch fringe: Start with a new length of conditioned thread and exit the bottom edge bead on either side of the base. String 20 cylinder beads, one 4mm pearl, and three 14º seeds. *Skip the three 14º seeds and go back through the pearl* (photo m and five cylinders. Pull snug to form a three-bead picot below the pearl. String five cylinders, one pearl, and three 14º seeds. Repeat from * to *. Go through five more beads on the base strand. Repeat this fringe twice more. Sew back up into the 8º bead that you exited at the beginning of this step.

2 Come down the next 8º bead and make another branched fringe.

3 Straight fringe: Weave over, skip one bead and exit the next 8º bead. String 20 cylinders, a 6mm crystal and three size 14ºs. Skip the 14ºs and go back through the rest of the beads on the fringe strand. Pull snug to form a three-bead picot below the crystal. Sew back into the 8º bead that you exited and come out the next 8º.

4 String 30 cylinders. Add branches along this strand as in step 1.

5 Center fringe: String 35 cylinders, a 6mm crystal, and three size 14ºs. Skip the 14ºs and go back up the rest of the beads. Pull tightly to form the picot below the crystal. Weave up into the next 8º to center the fringe on the base. Weave down through the next 8º bead.

6 Repeat step 4, 3, 2, and 1 to complete the other half of the fringe.

ADD THE PIN BACK
Start with a new length of conditioned thread. Position the pin back on the center back of the base, toward the top. Sew through the beads in the base and

the holes in the pin back to secure. Repeat this thread path several times for added security. Weave in the thread tails, knot, and glue.

MAKE THE NECKSTRAP
To turn the piece into a pendant, add a removable neck strap. You can purchase a neck strap or make one of your own. If you make it, you can match the colors to those in the brooch.

1 Start with 2 yd. (1.8m) of conditioned beading thread. Leave a 12-in. tail and work 16 in. (41cm) of spiral rope (see "Basics"). End with an 8º hex-cut or an 8º seed bead.

2 String eight 14º beads. Go back through the 8º bead added in step 1 to form a loop. Weave into the spiral rope and then back through the 8º and the 14ºs. Repeat this thread path several times for security. Repeat on the other end of the spiral rope.

3 Start a new doubled thread with a #12 needle. String an 8º and eight 14º beads. Go back through the 8º to form a loop. String a 2-in. (5cm) mixture of 6-8mm beads, pearls, and crystals. End by stringing an 8º and eight 14º beads. Go back through the 8º to form a loop. Tie several half hitches between beads and dab the knots with glue. Repeat to make a second strand.

4 Purchase or make four wire S-hooks. Attach the S-hooks to the neck straps and the loops on the pendant/pin as in the photo on p. 53.
– *Shantasa Saling*

MATERIALS
- 7.5g Japanese cylinder beads (Delicas), main color (MC)
- 3g Japanese cylinder beads (Delicas), accent color (AC)
- 5g size 14-15º seed beads, second accent color (AC), may all be one color or coordinating colors (edging and veins)
- 5g size 8º hex-cut seed beads
- assortment of 4mm and 6mm pearls, crystals, and rondelles
- Nymo D beading thread, color(s) to match
- beeswax or Thread Heaven
- beading needles, #10 or 12
- 1-in. (2.5cm) pin back
- G-S Hypo Cement or clear nail polish
- 4 wire S hooks, or 16-gauge round wire to make your own

BEADED BEADS

Lacy beaded beads

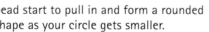

Some time ago, I thought I would make some beads out of beads. There was something humorous and redundant about the idea that appealed to me. I gave it a try, and this is one of the designs that evolved. Kathy Anderson, Carol Wilcox Wells, and Currie Butzbaugh have all helped me learn and enabled me to go off on my own tangent. I make the beads using peyote stitch in the round. They are hollow and the tension of the decreases keeps them stiff. After building the body of the bead, I embellish each with fringe, ruffles, lace, or whatever comes to mind.

I like to make color sets of five beads to combine with regular beads for a necklace. Often the colors remind me of flavors as I'm working, so the beads acquire names like blueberry pie à la mode, mint julep, cinnamon, etc. There are endless variations. Try making a really big bead out of size 11°s. Or with 48 beads as the base, make your first decrease at bead 7 instead of at bead 4. This produces a pyramid-shaped bead because the decreases fall in three places instead of four. You can make stripes of different widths or diamond and wedge shapes by using two or three colors in the original circle of 48. You can also make beads with an elongated or bullet shape by increasing the number of plain peyote rows worked between the decreases. Keep the tension firm, especially in the rows after each decrease. Give a firm tug at the decrease points, and you will see the

bead start to pull in and form a rounded shape as your circle gets smaller.

Work eleven rows of peyote stitch and then decrease for the first half of the bead. Then, flip the bead over and work the decrease rows for the second half. Next, attach the anchor beads, following the curved shape of the contrast color (CC) beads. Work diagonally across the midsection and around the CC curve on the other end. Bead the netted lace through the anchor beads and you're done! For a refresher on peyote stitch and how to decrease, see "Basics," p. 5.

MAKE THE BEAD

❶ Thread a needle with 2 yd. (1.8m) of conditioned Nymo. String 48 main color (MC) beads, leaving a 6-in. (15cm) tail. Tie the ends together with a square knot, forming a snug circle. Tie again for security.

❷ Cut a paper cup along the side seam to the bottom, trim off the bottom and the top rim and roll tightly to make a cone. Do not tape it closed. Slip your ring of 48 beads on the cone and let the cone expand (photo a).

❸ To begin the peyote stitch, go through the first bead to the left of the knot, (lefties, go the other way) pick up an MC bead, skip one bead, and go through the next bead. Continue around to the end of the circle. You have now completed row 3 (the original circle comprised rows 1 and 2). Go through the first beads of row 2 and row 3 (photo b). This is called the step-up because it steps your needle to a high bead to begin the next row. There are 24 beads in a row. Work 11 rows with a firm tension, and remove the beads from the paper cup.

❹ Begin decreasing on row 12. Work MC peyote stitch in the first four beads. Work the fifth bead but continue through the sixth bead without adding a bead (photo c). This is your first decrease. Using the CC beads, *work peyote stitch through the next four beads. Work the fifth and sixth beads together as before to make another decrease.* Using the MC beads, work from * to *. Finally repeat * to * using CC beads. You should now be at the end of the row, and it should have 20 beads.

❺ Notice that your bead is divided into four color sections. Work two rows in peyote stitch using the bead color that fits each section, no decreases. The last stitch of each section will go into the first bead in the next color group (photo d).

❻ For row 15, work the first three beads. Then work the fourth and fifth beads together to decrease. Continue around with the correct colors, working three beads and then decreasing in the fourth and fifth beads for each section. After the second decrease row, there will be 16 beads. Work the next two rows with the correct bead colors and no decreases.

❼ Decrease in each section for rows 18, 20, and 22. Work the rows between without decreases. When you reach the end, go through the beads on the end and pull them together. Make one or two half-hitch knots, dab them with nail polish, and take the thread through an adjacent bead. Don't cut off the tail; you'll need it for the trim.

❽ Flip the bead over, weave 2 yd. of waxed thread through the beadwork to anchor it, exiting the left side of the bead just to the right of the tail. Thread the starting tail onto a needle, weave it in, and trim both tails. Work steps 4 through 7 to decrease on the other side of the bead.

EMBELLISH THE BEAD

❶ Maneuver your needle to the second MC bead from the beaded bead's hole, next to the convex (arched) curve of a CC section, aiming it toward the middle of the beaded bead (photo e). Pick up

a

b

c

d

an anchor (AC) bead, skip an MC bead and go through the next MC bead. Continue adding AC beads, following the curve of the CC section. At the top of the CC section, add AC beads but move diagonally from right to left, across the midsection (photo f), and around the convex curve of the CC section on the other end until you reach the other end. Secure with a knot. Do not cut.

❷ Add two lace color (LC) beads, and go back through the AC bead you just added. Add three LC beads and go through the next AC bead. Continue to

e

f

g

MATERIALS

- size 15º seed beads in four colors—main (MC), contrast (CC), anchor (AC), and lace (LC)
- beading needle, #13
- Nymo B beading thread
- beeswax or Thread Heaven
- paper cup with waxed surface

the end. Next add one LC, one AC, and one LC bead, and go back through the middle LC bead in the previous row (photo g). Repeat around. Keep the tension tight so that the lace will stand up instead of flopping over. Add a third row of lace. This lace trim is slightly squishy but firm enough to withstand normal wear and tear.

❸ Repeat steps 1 and 2 of "embellish the bead" to add a swirl of lace to follow the other two CC sections.
– Rebecca Peapples

Bead around the bead

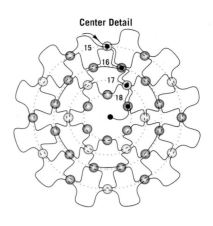

Center Detail

15
16
17
18

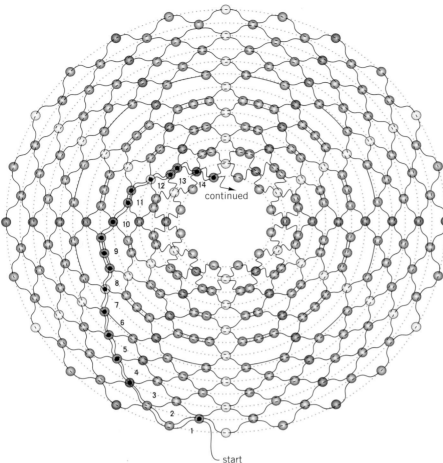

continued

12 13 14
11
10
9
8
7
6
5
4
3
2
1

start

MATERIALS

- 20mm round wooden bead
- Japanese cylinder beads, 5gm each of three colors (gold/silver-lined copper, matte black/matte gold, and ivory/alabaster)
- Nymo B or D beading thread, black
- beading needle, #10 or 12
- beeswax or Thread Heaven
- black indelible marker (or color to match main color bead)

The challenge of beaded beads is achieving balanced color and design on such a tiny surface. I usually choose six to eight colors before I start a bead, and I never graph my designs, which occur spontaneously as I work. I make beads of every size, shape, and combination of these colors that I can think of before moving on to other colors. For me, making these beaded beads remains endlessly fascinating.

The following pattern uses a limited color palette so you can learn my basic technique. When you feel comfortable with it, try making beads with your own colors and designs.

❶ Color the wooden bead completely with the marker. Run 5-6 ft. (1.52-1.83m) of thread through beeswax or Thread Heaven. Thread the needle single with no knot.

❷ Pick up one matte gold bead and move it to the end of the thread. Tie the first half of a square knot around the bead, leaving a ½-in. (1cm) tail. String two more gold beads, one copper, three gold, one alabaster, *three gold, one copper, three gold, one alabaster*. Repeat * to * four more times for a total of 48 beads. Pass the needle through the first bead (with the knot) then through the entire circle and two beads past the knot. The needle exits before the copper bead **(photo a)**.

❸ Work this row (the third) without the wooden bead in circular peyote stitch (see "Basics," p. 5) with the following color pattern: *one copper, one gold, one alabaster, one gold.* Repeat * to * five more times, adding a total of 24 beads. To start row 4, take the needle through the last bead in the previous row and the first bead added in this row for the step up.

❹ Making sure the knot and the tail are on the underside of the circle, carefully slide the beadwork onto the ball to the middle where it fits most snugly **(photo b)**. If the beadwork is stretched too tight, start over and choose larger cylinder beads for the foundation. *(Note: even though Japanese cylinder beads are uniform, you'll notice some size variation that you can exploit to make your designs*

a

b

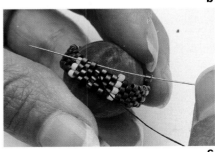

c

work.) Throughout the construction of this bead, choose beads that comfortably fill the spaces without crowding the work. The goal is to have as little thread show as possible without bumping the beads up out of place. Don't worry about being precisely in the middle at this point. Snip the tail to about ¼ in. (6mm).

❺ Working gently so you don't dislodge the beadwork, add only gold beads on row 4. Let the needle or the bead hang periodically to release the twist that will develop.
Work row 5: one gold, one alabaster, one gold, one copper; repeat the pattern five more times. Make sure the tail stays flat and under the beadwork. Use only gold beads on row 6.

❻ Begin row 7 with *one alabaster bead then decrease by running the needle through the next two gold beads; add one copper and decrease again **(photo c)**.* Repeat * to * five more times—12 beads added.

❼ Zigzag the needle through the beadwork to exit the other side of the foundation row **(photo d)**.

❽ Repeat steps 5 and 6 on this side, making sure that the pattern lines up symmetrically.

❾ Now center the beadwork on the bead as exactly as possible. The next two steps will commit you to this placement, which will determine how even the holes will be.

❿ Work row 8, placing three very short gold beads in each large space **(photo e)**. If three beads won't fit, fill the spaces with two somewhat larger beads instead.

⓫ Sew back to the other side and repeat step 10.

⓬ Work row 9, alternating one copper and one alabaster and going through each group of gold beads as a single bead **(photo f)**. From now on, repeat each row on the other side before working the next row.

⓭ Work row 10 with two gold beads in each large space.

⓮ Work row 11 in the same pattern as row 9.

⓯ Work row 12 in the same pattern as row 10.

⓰ Work row 13 as row 9.

⓱ Work row 14 with one gold bead in each space **(photo g)**.

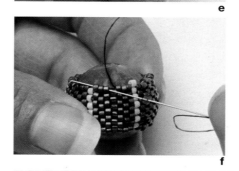

When the thread starts to run short, end it by zigzagging back through the work. Go around a thread between two beads and tie a half hitch knot **(photo h)**. Go through two to three more beads and pull the knot inside the first bead. Holding the thread taut, cut it as close to the last bead as possible, and the end will pop back into the bead. Begin a new thread by zigzagging through two to three beads several rows before the last. Knot as before. Then zigzag through the work to the point where you stopped.

⓲ Work row 15 as row 9.

⓳ Work row 16 as row 14.

⓴ Work row 17 adding one alabaster bead and going through two beads on the previous row (you'll be skipping the copper beads with this decrease)—six beads added.

㉑ Work row 18 with one copper bead in each space. Then go back through the six copper beads added on this row to reinforce it **(photo i)**. After repeating this row on the other side, end the thread by weaving it in as described above.

– Sharri Moroshok

Wonder beads unveiled

Learn to design and embellish these hollow, peyote-stitch gems in just about any design you can imagine. Once you can make the two basic shapes shown here, you'll be ready to experiment with other shapes, sizes, and colors. Have fun!

Make Wonder Beads using circular peyote for the body section, then decrease sharply and add smaller peyote tubes at each end. Embellishing the surface stiffens the bead and reinforces its structure.

BASIC WONDER BEAD

❶ Start the circular peyote body by stringing 32 main color (MC) beads. Tie the tail and working thread together with a square knot (see "Basics," p. 5) to make a circle, leaving a 6-in. (15cm) tail to weave in later. These beads make up rows 1 and 2.

❷ Work nine more rows of circular peyote (see "Basics") for a total of 11 rows. (A 32-bead tube fits comfortably around a fat Sharpie marker.) Keep the tension tight as you work; the peyote body should be stiff. Step up as if you were about to start row 12 **(photo a).**

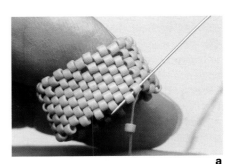

a

❸ With your thread exiting a bead on row 11, string on one accent color (AC) and one MC bead. Turn, and go back through the AC bead to make a "spike." Go through the next two beads

b

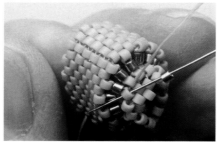

d

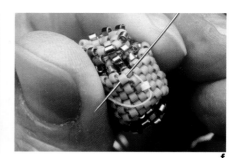

f

c

e

g

(figure, opposite page) in the same direction as in step 2. Repeat, making a total of 16 spikes. When you complete the last spike, work the thread back to the main-color bead at the end of that spike (photo b).

❹ Take the needle through the main color beads on all 16 spikes to form a tight circle. Go through the circle of beads a second time and tie a half-hitch knot (see "Basics") within the work to secure the circle. These beads become the base for another section of circular peyote. Stitch through the next bead to avoid starting at the knot. Work three additional rows of circular peyote to form a five-row cuff (photo c).

❺ Work the thread back through several cuff beads until it exits an MC bead at the end of a spike in row 2. Pick up an AC bead, skip an end bead, and stitch through the next end bead (photo d). Continue until you have eight AC beads in this row.

❻ Work diagonally through one bead to begin the next row and add AC beads as before. This row of beads will be offset from the first. Work through to the next row and add another row of AC beads. Before cutting the thread, weave through several beads to secure it. This layer of beads looks like a checkerboard (photo e).

❼ Add thread on the bead's other side and repeat steps 3-6, but don't cut the thread when you're done.

❽ Stitch back through the cuff and spikes and exit from a bead in the

second to the last row on the body section (not the row connected to spikes). Pick up an AC bead and stitch through the next bead in that row (photo f). Complete the row, adding a total of 16 accent beads.

❾ Skip a row by stitching diagonally through two beads. Add AC beads as in step 8. These beads line up with the beads in the first row.

❿ Add three more rows of AC beads (photo g). Weave the thread through several beads before cutting.

SAUCER-SHAPED WONDER BEAD

❶ Follow steps 1-8 above, working seven rows of circular peyote for the body instead of 11.

❷ After completing the first row of AC beads (step 8, above), stitch diagonally to the next row. Add another row of AC beads. These beads will be offset from the ones in the previous row. Stitch these two rows together by zigzagging between beads (photo h). Once the rows are stitched together, they look like two rows of peyote on top of the main color.

❸ Work two rows of peyote off the accent beads added in step 2. These rows are not attached to the bead's body. Sew back into the body and work the fifth row the same as accent row 1, stitching through the next-to-last row of the body section. When complete, stitch this row to row 4, as in step 2.

❹ With the thread exiting a bead in row 4, use MC beads to add three

embellishment rows over layer 2. Stitch them together tightly by zigzagging between beads (photo i). Because the circumference of the bead has increased, use the largest of the beads for these outer layers.

❺ To make the final layer, stitch two accent beads into each space along the center row of MC beads added in step 4. Then add single accent beads in the remaining spaces (photo j).

– Sue Jackson and Wendy Hubick

h

j

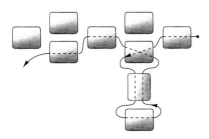

i

MATERIALS

- Japanese cylinder beads: main color and two accent colors
- Nymo D or Silamide beading thread
- beeswax or Thread Heaven for Nymo
- beading needles, #12

VARIATIONS ON THE BASIC WONDER BEADS

• When designing your own Wonder Beads, start with an even number of beads divisible by four. A 32-bead diameter is a good size to embellish, but larger Wonder Beads have space for more intricate patterns.

• For a symmetrical bead, you must have an uneven number of rows in the body.

• When making the spike, substitute a size 1 bugle or two cylinder beads for the AC bead. This changes the bead's profile from a compact shape to a more elongated one.

• Do as many spike decrease rows in a bead as you'd like. For example, if you start with a 48-bead body, you can decrease to 24 beads, then to 12 beads, and even six beads. Cuffs between spike decreases need at least three rows.

• The stabilizing layer, although decorative, is very important for making Wonder Beads stiff enough to keep their shapes.

• For the embellishment layer, try 2mm beads. Semi-precious stones, glass, and precious metals work well when they are not too closely spaced.

Beaded
buttons

The principle for covering a button form in peyote stitch is similar to making a beaded bead. You start at the widest point of the circumference and work decreases to close the beadwork at the center. The trick with the button is to work with small enough beads to create an interesting pattern and to use the decreases to help shape the pattern without bulges or gaps.

Test the beads for colorfastness in hot water and laundry detergent if you plan to wash the buttons. It's safer, however, to attach these buttons with button pins and remove them before washing or dry cleaning. Beads that are washfast may not be colorfast when subject to dry cleaning solvents.

Cover the button forms smoothly in quilter's-weight cotton or polyester/cotton. Use a solid color or a small-scale print. Almost no fabric will show. Then sew a ring of seed beads one at a time around the edge of the button. Work peyote stitch into this base round. Decrease when the beadwork reaches the top side of the button. Decreases will become more frequent as you near the center. Make more buttons, experimenting with patterns and the decrease placement.

If the first round of sewn beads is an even number (24 in these patterns), you will have a step-up; if there are an odd number, you won't, and you'll be able to do spirals of patterns. For different size beads or button forms, you will have to determine the best number of beads around the edge, the most effective number of decreases per round, and the appropriate frequency of decreases. Decreases look best if they're spaced evenly. I find that six or seven per round work well. Plan the starting number of beads to be divisible by the number of decreases. As a rule of thumb, if your beadwork bulges, you need to work a decrease round at this point or on the round before. For circular peyote stitch and rapid decreasing, see "Basics," p. 5.

❶ Thread a beading needle with about 1 yd. (.9m) of Nymo or Silamide and take a small backstitch on the top of the button form to secure the thread (**photo a, p. 68**). Bring the thread under

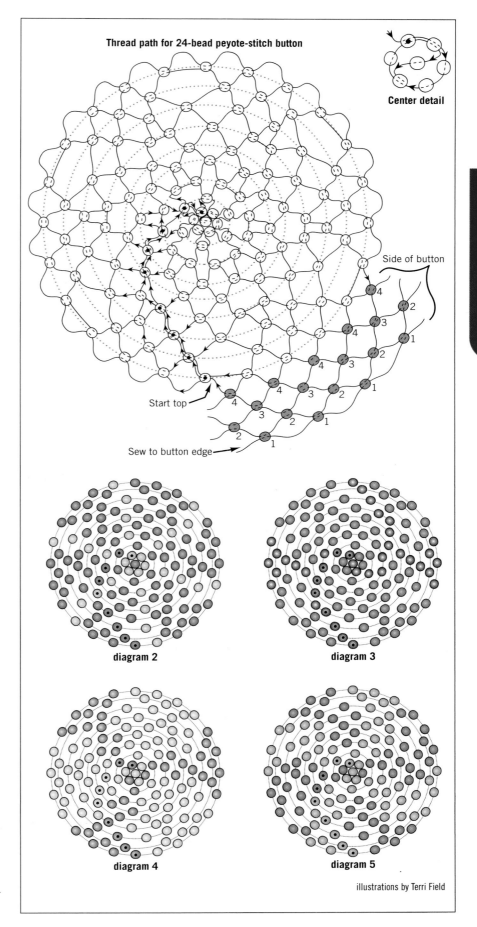

Thread path for 24-bead peyote-stitch button

Center detail

Side of button

Start top

Sew to button edge

diagram 2

diagram 3

diagram 4

diagram 5

illustrations by Terri Field

the cloth with several stitches and exit near the bottom edge.

❷ Sew one orange seed bead onto the cloth at the bottom edge with the hole parallel to the edge of the button. Bring the needle back out half a bead space beyond the first bead. Repeat around (photo b) for 24 beads, ending with a small space between the last and first beads of the row. Go through the first bead.

❸ Pick up one blue bead and begin peyote stitching by going through the second orange bead (photo c). Continue peyote stitching around (rows 2 and 4 blue, row 3 orange) until the beadwork is level with the edge of the button top (four rows—photo d).

❹ Work the first round of the top without decreasing. Follow diagram 2 on p. 67. Dots on beads indicate the first bead of the row. See the top diagram for the thread path.

❺ For the first decrease round, work three stitches and one decrease six times—18 blue beads. Decrease by bringing the needle through two high beads instead of one (photo e).

❻ Work the next two rounds normally. Put one bead in the space where you went through two on the row below (photo f)—18 beads.

❼ Decrease on the next round: go through two beads and add an orange; go through one bead and add a blue. Repeat around six times—12 beads. Work the next two rounds without decreasing. Photo g shows the last stitch, orange, and the step-up, which is a bit more involved than usual. You must step up through three beads rather than two.

❽ On the last decrease round, decrease each pair of stitches into one —six blue. Work a final round with six orange beads. Then go through the six beads to pull them together. Exit any center bead and string one blue or orange bead to fill the hole. Enter the bead opposite the one you exited from the opposite direction (photo h). Weave the thread through beads, then under the cloth, and out the side to end it.
– David Chatt

a

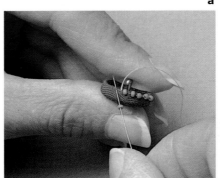

b

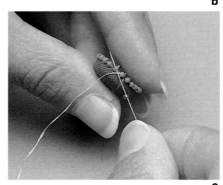

c

d

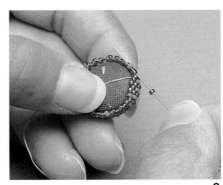

e

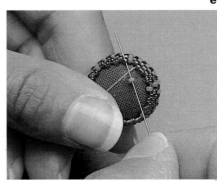

f

g

h

MATERIALS

- size 14º Czech or size 15º Japanese seed beads in two colors (blue and orange)
- ⅝-in. covered button forms (slightly dome-shaped)
- scrap of cotton or polyester/cotton fabric (2 square. in. per button)
- beading needle, #12 or 13
- Nymo B or Silamide beading thread to match darker bead

AMULET BAGS

Medicine bags

Jennifer Clement developed a series of unique mandala designs for her amulet bags. Each one appears, at first glance, to be a snowflake. But when you look closer, they are actually representational images. Besides the four designs that are re-created here, she has many others available through her bead store. Read on to learn about her methods for making her bags.

I've been a beader since I was a child. During the late '60s when beads were really in, my parents bought me a bead loom. I didn't like the loom, but I loved the beads and started dragging my parents everywhere to look for beads. Now after making my living doing beadwork in one way or another, I co-own Beadweaver, a bead store in Santa Fe, and my life continues to be oriented around beads.

I like to make these medicine bags or amulet purses to commemorate major events. I design a six-pointed "snowflake" design or a mandala for each purse. Look closely and you will see that each design is actually representative. **Figure 1** at right is called Turtles Dancing, Frogs and Ladybugs Keeping Watch. The one below it, **figure 2**, is called Angels. **Figures 4** and **5** on p. 74 are Tree-star and Lotus Flower. The design on the white amulet purse on p. 70 was made for the midwife who delivered my son. It was the first snowflake design I created, and it shows six women giving birth.

CREATING A DESIGN

I've tried to make these designs with eight points, but they never turned out very well. I think peyote stitch just orients well to a six-sided design. An important consideration when designing a purse is to use colors with high contrast. This makes the design pop. I recommend using a light background and bright or dark colors which will hold the details of the design. Or use a black background and light colors for another type of high-contrast look.

CENTERING A DESIGN

These designs are symmetrical, just like real snowflakes. Therefore, they require an odd count of vertical rows: a central row with an equal number of

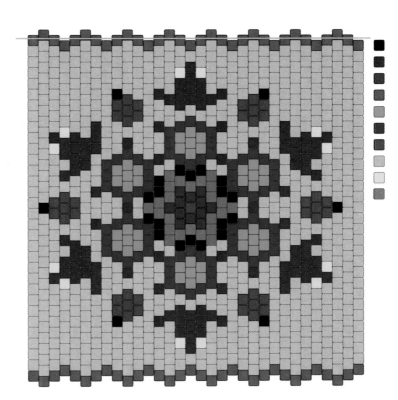

figure 1

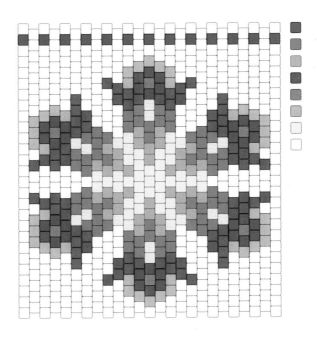

figure 2

rows on both sides. Because I don't like to work on flat peyote pieces, I make all my purses with circular peyote. However, the bags must lay flat when complete, so you must have an equal number of vertical rows for the front and back sides. This works fine when you put a design on the front and stitch a solid-color back side. But I don't find continuous monochromatic stitching very interesting, so I like to put the design on both sides.

You must consider certain parameters when making a bag with an odd number of vertical peyote rows on each side. If you have 25 vertical rows in your design, you will have a circular bag with 50 vertical rows. Because of the "up" and "down" orientation of peyote rows, each side will only have a center bead every other row and those rows will not be the same on both sides. In brief, you will have to start the pattern on the back side one horizontal row above or below the one on the front side. You just have to remember to make that adjustment when you are stitching the purse.

Another option is to place your design a little off-center by adding another vertical row to each side. If you have 26 or any even number of vertical rows on each side of the bag, there is no "central" row. My Birth amulet bag and my Turtles Dancing design both are made with this adjustment. There are two vertical rows of background color on the right side of each design and only one on the left side. When it comes time to zip up the bottom of the bag and to fringe the sides of the bag, you can finesse this "uneven" situation by laying the bag so the side edge is actually a vertical row of beads. By subtracting the extra row from each side, you are back to having an uneven number of rows and the design will be centered. When you add fringe to the sides, you must add it to both edges of the beads on the side vertical rows to cover all exposed thread.

STITCHING THE BAG

Follow one of my patterns or create your own design. Decide whether to use seed beads or cylinder beads for the body of the bag. I started out making my bags with 22º and 24º seed beads,

but now I use Japanese cylinder beads. The holes are much easier to see, many colors are available, and the uniform size creates a nice bead fabric.

The first few rows of peyote are always the most difficult. To make the start easier, I often use a contrast color for the first or third row. This makes it much easier to see where to put the beads for the fourth row and prevents twisting the rows at the beginning.

❶ Thread a needle with a 1-yd. (.9m) length of Nymo. String the required number of beads to complete the first two rows of your chosen design, leaving a 6-in. tail. Since this bag will be stitched in even-count circular peyote (see "Basics," p. 5), you must remember to pick enough beads for the front as well as the back. This will be an even number of beads.

❷ Tie the two thread ends together with a square knot (see "Basics"), leaving some ease.

❸ To begin row 3, go through the first bead to the left of the knot. Pick up the first row 3 bead, skip a bead, and go through the next bead. Continue around in this manner until you get to the end of row 3.

❹ Because you are doing even-count circular peyote, you will "step up" at the end of each row from here on out. To step up for row 4, go through the first bead of rows 2 and 3. Pick up the first row 4 bead and go through the second row 3 bead. Continue around in this manner to complete row 4. If you find that you don't step up and you start spiraling instead, stop and check your work for a missed bead.

❺ Continue working in even-count circular peyote to complete the body of the bag.

ZIPPING UP THE BOTTOM

Once the body of the bag is complete, excluding any edging at the top, stitch up the bottom of the bag. Lay the bag flat with the pattern centered and sew between the "up" beads on back and front bottom edges (see "Basics" and photo a).

TOP EDGING

I almost always make a row of points along the top edge of the bag's back side. The smallest points, shown in the Turtles design on p. 71, are made by adding only the beads above the orange line on the diagram, as follows:

❶ Sew out an "up" bead next to the back edge. *Add a bead, sew through the next "up" bead (photo b), go into the following "down" bead, and continue through the next "up" bead.* Repeat from * to * to add points along the back edge (or around the entire edge if you prefer).

The larger points on the 50-count bags, shown in the large bag on p. 70, are made by adding two groups of five-row peaks, as follows:

❷ Add five beads in a row between "up" beads along the back edge. Skip a space by going into the next "down" bead and through the next "up" bead (photo c) and add five more beads.

❸ To add the next row of beads, you'll have to get your needle into position so that it exits the last bead added in the opposite direction. To do so, after adding the last bead in your new row, loop around the thread connecting the two beads immediately below the bead you just added and go back through it (figure 3, opposite page).

❹ Add beads between the new "up" beads, with one bead fewer in each row (photo d) to create a point (photo e). Make the turn following figure 3 for each new row.

❺ After adding the single bead for the last row, sew back through the beadwork and finish off the thread with a few half-hitch knots (see "Basics") between beads.

❻ If you wish, embellish the points by stringing some beads between them as shown in photo f.

TAB CLOSURE

A simple closure is the best way to ensure security without distracting from the design. First, sew a round bead to the center top on the front side of your bag. Now, choose one of the following methods for making the loop closure.

If you want a simple loop and bead closure, like the one pictured on p. 70, sew out from a bead at the purse's center back. String a size 6º or 8º bead

a

b

c

d

e

f

g

h

figure 3

MATERIALS

- size 11º Japanese cylinder beads in a variety of colors
- 1–3 size 6º or 8º seed beads for clasp
- assorted seed beads and larger beads for fringe and strap
- Nymo D or B beading thread
- beeswax or Thread Heaven
- beading needles, #10 or 12

and enough seed beads to fit around the bead or button you're using for the closure. Sew back into the 6º or 8º bead in the opposite direction and end your thread securely in the purse's beadwork with a few half-hitch knots.

Alternatively, attach your loop to a three-bead-wide tab sewn in ladder stitch (see "Basics"), as follows:

❶ Make a loop of seed beads which will fit your closure button or bead and sew through the loop of beads again.

❷ String three beads, go through the last three beads on the loop, and go back through the three beads just added again in the same direction. String three more beads, go through the beads in the row below and back through the beads just added. Make four or five total rows of ladder stitch and then attach the ladder to the inside back edge of the purse (photo g).

BOTTOM FRINGE

I'm persnickety about fringe and often pull it out if it doesn't meet my standards. I like to make two rows of fringe that taper back evenly from a long center fringe. I use a variety of seed beads, gemstones, pearls, drop beads, and charms. I add one fringe row from the front bottom of the bag, stringing a fringe from every other bead across the row (photo h). Then I add a matching row to the bottom back of the bag, also skipping every other bead.

LACY SIDE EDGING

Trim the side edges before adding a necklace strap. I add two lines of three-bead picots along the front and back sides to hide the bead holes that show when the bag lies flat.

❶ Sew out a bead at the bottom of the bag's front side. *Pick up three 14º seed beads and sew into the next bead along the edge (photo i, p. 74).

❷ Turn and sew out the next bead (photo j, p. 74).*

❸ Repeat from * to * along the entire front edge, turn, and repeat along the back side edge (photo k, p. 74), covering the bead holes of both vertical peyote rows on the purse's side (photo l, p. 74). If you decided to use one vertical row on each side of the bag, remember to fringe on both sides of the edge beads to cover exposed thread.

NECKLACE STRAP

Use seed beads, larger accent beads, and pearls to make a necklace strap.

❶ Cut a length of Nymo six times the desired length of the necklace strap and thread it on a needle doubled.

❷ Sew into the body of the purse, leaving a 4-in. (10cm) tail, and zigzag through the beads to exit the end bead on the top front edge.

❸ String the necklace strap as desired

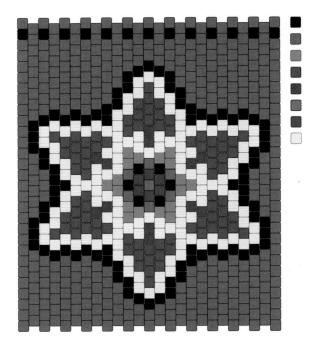

figure 4

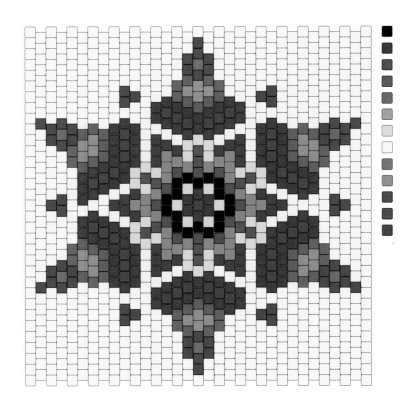

figure 5

i

j

k

l

(make sure it is long enough to go over your head).

4 Sew into the end bead on the opposite front corner, turn, and come out the end bead on the back corner.

5 Sew back through the beads on the necklace strap and into the end bead on the opposite back corner. Zigzag through the beadwork of the body to secure the thread and trim both tails close to the beads.

– *Jennifer Clement*

Tribute to the rain forest

Every spring tadpoles appear in puddles and small pools and gradually turn into frogs. As a child growing up in Australia, I loved watching their metamorphosis. I am still intrigued by frogs, and I wanted to design a purse with a stylized frog design. So my artist friend, Karla Englehardt, and I graphed a frog for an odd-count, flat peyote bag.

We used flat peyote to eliminate a bottom seam, and odd-count allowed us to center the frog motif and create a symmetrically decreased triangular flap. The purse is suitable for beginning to intermediate beaders. But a number of special touches add interest for most levels of bead workers: I used Jack Frost™, a hydrofluoric acid solution, to etch the background beads so the jewel-like shiny beads of the frog stand out against the muted background. The reined fringe along the sides is an effect I've never seen before—a large bead at the base of each fringe holds it firmly in place so it covers the seam and doesn't droop. I approached the design of the strap as a true necklace that would accentuate the mood of the bag. The purse is also larger than any I've seen—3 in. high by 2¾ in. wide. It's not quite tall enough for a credit card, but I'll remedy that on the next one. Feel free to revise my pattern to make your bag bigger if you wish.

The purse body is a single long rectangle, approximately 7 in. by 2³⁄₄ in. (16 x7cm), worked in odd-count flat peyote stitch. Many people avoid this stitch because figuring out how to add the last bead on the odd-numbered rows can be tricky. However, the method shown below is easy and foolproof. I'll also show you a new kind of horizontal fringe. For flat peyote technique, see "Basics," p. 5.

THE BODY

❶ Thread the needle and then cut a 1 yd. (.9m) length of Nymo. Tie a temporary stop bead to the end of the thread and leave a 4-6 in. (10-15cm) tail. The stop bead holds the beads of the base row together (remove it after working a few rows).

❷ Using the chart on p. 78 as a guide and starting with bead 1, string the 45 beads of the base row (rows 1 and 2) as indicated by the numbers.

❸ Working from right to left and reading the chart from right to left, pick up the first bead of row 3. Pass the needle back through bead 44 on the base row. Pick up the next bead of row 3 and pass the needle through bead 42, and so on.

❹ The major obstacle with odd-count, flat peyote is that at the end of each odd-numbered row, there is no bead to which you can anchor the last bead. For row 3 only (all the others are easy), you need to bring the thread through a figure-8 pattern to anchor the last bead, as follows: Pick up the last bead of row 3 and take the needle through bead 1, up through bead 2, and down through bead 3. Then come up through the next-to-last bead of row 3, back through bead 2, then 1, and finally around the edge and through the last bead on row 3. Begin row 4.

❺ Turn the beadwork over so you can keep working from right to left, but read the chart from left to right on even-numbered rows. You'll have no trouble anchoring the last bead of all even-numbered rows.

❻ From row 5 on, anchor the thread at the end of odd-numbered rows by

looping around the edge thread between the two rows below as shown in **photo a**. Then come back through the end bead **(photo b)**. Continue until approximately 6 in. (15cm) of thread remains.

❼ To join the old working thread to a new length of thread, tie a knot in the end of the new thread and zigzag through the woven beads, coming out the same bead as the old thread in the same direction. Gently tug the knot into a bead. Using a square knot, tie the threads together as close as possible. Complete a few more rows with the new thread. Then zigzag the tail of the old thread into the beadwork. Finish beading up to the flap.

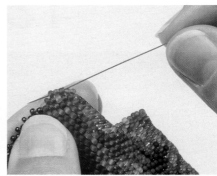

THE FLAP

❶ To begin, either zigzag the thread over to where the flap begins or start a new thread. Weave the first 13 rows of the flap in odd-count peyote

❷ Decrease the flap edges by stopping one bead short at the beginning and end of each row, looping the thread around the edge thread between the two rows below, as shown in **photos c-e**. Add the last bead on a decrease, bring the needle through the last bead on each of the two rows before (only one row on first decrease) **(photo c)**. Loop the thread around the threads below the second bead **(photo d)**. Then turn the work over and bring the needle through those two beads again (three

g

j

h

k

i

l

MATERIALS

- size 11º seed beads:
  - **2 hanks** transparent multi-colored "tortoise" amber (don't use the darkest amber beads) OR use **1 hank** very pale amber, **1 hank** light amber, and **1 hank** medium amber
  - **hank** transparent dark green
  - **190** opaque dark lavender
  - **112** transparent light green
  - **28** metallic copper colored
- **60** size 8º seed beads, medium amber
- assorted larger beads
- **2** 12mm bead caps
- Nymo D or B beading thread, beige or white
- beeswax or Thread Heaven
- beading needles, #10 or 12
- GS Hypo Cement

Optional: Jack Frost™ hydrofluoric acid to etch the amber and lavender beads to a matte finish (available at bead stores; or use a less hazardous product called Glass Bead Etching Crème available from Arrow Springs, www.arrowsprings.com, (800) 899-0689)— follow safety precautions.

thread passes through them) and through the last bead added **(photo e)**. Pick up the first bead for the next row. Continue decreasing until one bead is left. Then zigzag back through the beadwork and clip the thread.

SIDE SEAMS

Fold the starting edge of the purse up so that points A and C meet points B and D on the **chart** on p. 78. Starting at the top, align the beads of each side and weave the sides together. Work from top to bottom then back up to the top. Sew under the edge threads **(photo f)**, rather than whipping over them, to keep the seam from being too tight and puckering the side. Knot the ends, together; repeat on the other side.

FRINGE

First choose obscuring beads wide enough to hide the side seam. Most of my obscuring beads are a stack of two to three contemporary metal heishi beads from Kenya (I also used a few other miscellaneous beads to get the varied, ethnic look I wanted). In this method, two short, approximately ½ in. (1.3cm), fringes come out of each obscuring bead, and the obscuring beads are strung along the seam with their edges touching.

❶ Working from the top, anchor the thread so it comes from the far side of the seam, passing under all the seam threads and out the front **(photo g)**. String the obscuring bead(s) and the beads of the first fringe. Use small

seed beads for the first ¼ in. (6mm) of each fringe.

❷ Take the thread back through all but the end bead, including the obscuring bead(s). Bring the needle under the side seam threads from back to front of the purse **(photo h)**.

❸ Bring the needle back through the obscuring bead **(photo i)** and string the second fringe. Go back into the same obscuring bead, coming out toward the front of the purse. Bringing the needle through both sides of the seam for each pair of fringes centers the obscuring bead over the seam.

❹ Continue fringing until the sides are covered. For an ethnic look, vary the fringe ends by using unusual beads and by stringing some fringes with pendant ends.

FINISHING TOUCHES

❶ Braid three strands of seed beads, including one strand of size 8º seed beads and hang them from the bottom

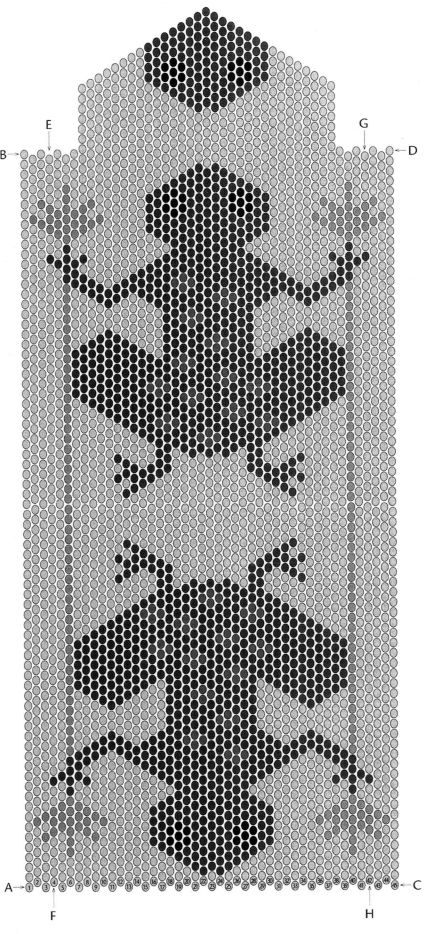

corners of the purse, like a swag, coming out of large obscuring beads (I used small glass donuts). Hang a charm or dangle from the swag's center with a wrapped loop (see "Basics"). I used a dragonfly assembled with beads and wire.

❷ String a bridge of six size 8° seed beads between the front and back edges of the purse between point E and F and G and H on the chart **(photo j).** This allows the purse to open wide and centers the weight. Anchor the bridge securely and sew back through the beads once or twice. You attach the strap to the center of the bridges.

❸ Pick a length for the necklace/strap and lay out the beads. Use doubled thread (heavy single thread is shown here for clarity) and knot securely to the center of one bridge. Glue the knot with GS Hypo Cement. Begin stringing with a bead cap placed so the cap covers the knot. When you finish stringing the necklace, end with another bead cap **(photo k).** Bring the necklace cord through the bridge, then back through the bead cap and the end bead. Knot between beads **(photo l, p. 77).** Go through a few more beads and knot again. Glue the knots and trim the tail.
– *Nicolette Stessin*

HOME DÉCOR

Collectible catch-alls

Enjoy the bright colors and tailored look of these diminutive baskets that feature geometric designs taken from woven plaids and quilt blocks. Use them to hold rings or to display tiny flowers or small candies. In holiday colors, they make wonderful ornaments.

PLAID BASKET—BODY

Each row consists of a six-bead pattern that repeats six times. The design needs to be well-defined, so choose colors with high contrast.

❶ String 72 main-color beads onto 4 ft. (1.2m) of waxed thread. Tie the beads into a circle with a square knot (see "Basics," p. 5), leaving a 6-in. (15cm) tail to weave in later. Allow a little ease in the bead ring. These beads comprise the basket's first two rows.

❷ Slip your work over a cardboard form, if desired. Using the main-color

beads, add two rows of circular peyote (see "Basics").

❸ Follow the basket pattern in **figure 1**, starting at the "x" at lower right. Repeat the pattern three times per row. To inset a design, as shown in the blue basket, substitute a pattern from **figure 2** for the section outlined in **figure 1**.

HANDLE

❶ Thread the needle with about a yard (.9m) of waxed Nymo and use it doubled. Secure the thread in several beads in the basket's top rows. If you've worked the inset design, center it when you attach the handle; otherwise, start the handle anywhere along the top row. Stitch two-bead rows in flat peyote (see "Basics") for 2¼ in. (5.7cm). Attach the handle to the top row of beads on the opposite side of the basket.

❷ Stitch back through the beads in

the handle to stiffen it. (As the beads fill with thread, it will get harder to pass the needle through them. Use chainnose pliers or a rubber jar opener to grip and turn the needle slightly to ease it through, but don't force it or you may break a bead.) Weave the threads into the beadwork before cutting.

NETTED LACE BOTTOM

❶ String 12 beads and tie them into a circle, leaving a 6-in. tail (figure 3a). Go through the first bead.

❷ String three beads and go through the third bead in the circle (figure 3b). String another three beads and go through the fifth bead. Repeat until you've made a six-pointed star. Go through two beads on the first three-bead point.

❸ String five beads. Go through the center bead of the next point (**figure 3c**). Make five more points. Go through three beads along the first five-bead point.

❹ String seven beads. Go through the center bead of the next point (**figure 3d**). Make five more points. Go through four beads along the first seven-bead point.

❺ String nine beads. Go through the center bead of the next point (**figure 3e**). Make five more points. Go through four beads along the first nine-bead point.

❻ To attach the lace bottom to the basket, go through any "up" bead in the first row of the main section. Skip the fifth (center) bead, go into the sixth, and exit at the fourth bead on the next point (**figure 4**).

❼ Skip five "up" beads on the basket's first row and go through the sixth. Repeat until all six points of the bottom are attached to the basket. Weave the thread tails into the beadwork.

TUMBLING BLOCKS BASKET

❶ String 80 beads, tie them into a circle, and follow the pattern in **figure 5**, repeating the pattern twice per row.

❷ When you reach the basket's top edge, work each diamond's upper half in flat peyote stitch.

❸ Increase the size of the netted bottom to fit this basket as follows: After making the last point in step 5, above, go through five beads along the first nine-bead point. String 11 beads. Go through the center of the next point. Make five more points. Exit through the fifth bead along the first 11-bead point.

❹ To attach the bottom, follow the directions in steps 6 and 7, above, skipping the sixth (center) bead along the points. When you connect the points to the main basket section, skip six "up" beads four times and five "up" beads twice. – *Sue Swanson*

MATERIALS
- **3–4** tubes of Japanese cylinder beads, main color and two or three accent colors
- Nymo D beading thread to match the main-color beads
- beeswax or Thread Heaven
- beading needles, #10 or #10 sharps
- cardboard tube (optional)

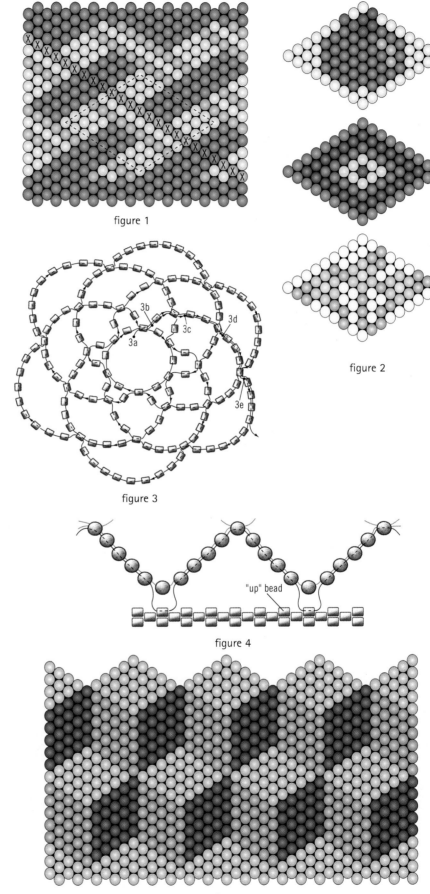

figure 1

figure 2

figure 3

figure 4

"up" bead

figure 5

HOME DÉCOR

Beaded tassels

Liven up a tassel with a peyote-stitched beaded tassel cover. It's a great way for beginners to learn peyote while following a pattern, but it also encourages experimenting with different finishing techniques.

The tassels stand alone as ornaments to hang on a drawer knob or make a great fob for your favorite pair of embroidery scissors. Try different fibers for the tassel—rayon, silk, metallic thread. So many possibilities exist.

Follow the pattern for a peyote band. Zip up the beadwork and add loops or fringe to each end. Make a tassel with a beaded loop for hanging. Slide the tassel through the beaded tube and stitch it in place.

PEYOTE TUBE

❶ Arrange the Japanese cylinder beads by color into three small piles on your beading surface. Assign each color a letter (A, B, C).

❷ Cut a 2-yd. (1.8m) length of beading thread. String a stop bead 8 in. (20cm) from the end of the thread and go through the bead again in the same direction. The stop bead will prevent your beads from falling off until you have completed several rows of peyote.

❸ String eight seed beads in the following order: A, A, B, B, C, C, A, A (rows 1 and 2). Following the diagonal stripe pattern below, work in even-count peyote (see "Basics," p. 5) for 36 rows, making a total of six diagonals for each color—18 beads on each end.

❹ Remove the stop bead. Fold the beadwork in half so the first and last rows are side by side and "zip up" the ends (see "Basics" and **photo a**). Set aside the thread and needle.

❺ Thread a needle on the 8 in. tail. Pass the needle down through the bead from which the thread you set aside in step 4 exits and secure these last two beads **(photo b)**. Tie a half-hitch knot (see "Basics") between the beads and weave the tail back and forth through the beadwork several times

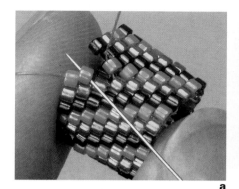

a

b

c

d

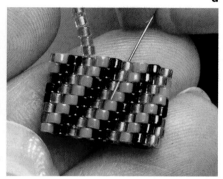

e

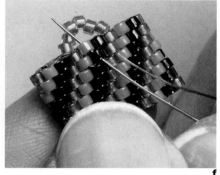

f

to secure it. Trim the tail as close to the beads as possible.

LOOPS AND FRINGE

Three different techniques were used to embellish the top and bottom of the tassels (see photo, p. 82). The bottom of the blue tassel and the top of the red and black tassels are densely packed loops. The top of the blue tassel and the bottom of the black tassel are simple loops. The bottom of the red tassel has fringe that ends with a drop bead. For each technique described, string beads the same color as the peyote bead from which the thread exits. If your thread is getting short, end it and start a new thread.

SIMPLE LOOPS

❶ For top loops, string six beads on the remaining thread and go down

through the third bead to the right—the same color bead **(photo c)**.

❷ Bring the needle up through the first bead to the left **(photo d)**. Repeat all the way around the top edge of the peyote tube. As you begin each loop, keep the thread in front of the previous loop.

❸ For bottom simple loops, string 24 beads for each loop.

DENSELY PACKED LOOPS

❶ For top loops, string six beads and go down through the third bead to the right (same color) and the bead diagonally to the left below it **(photo e)**.

❷ Pass through the bead to the left and diagonally through the bead above so your needle is coming out the end bead next to the beginning of the loop **(photo f)**. As you add beads for a new loop, keep the start of each loop in

g

j

l

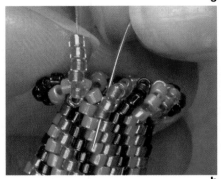

h

k

m

i

front of the previous loop (photo g). When you reach where the loops started, end the new loop behind the loop to the right (photo h).

❸ For bottom dense loops, string 12 beads for each loop.

FRINGE

❶ String 12 beads and a small drop bead. Skip the drop and go back up through the fringe beads. Reenter the end bead of the peyote tube that you exited (photo i).

❷ Bring the needle down through the next end bead and repeat step 1.

TASSEL

❶ Remove the paper bands from the skein of floss. Cut a 12-in. (31cm) length of floss from the skein.

❷ Leaving the skein of floss intact, tie the cut length of floss around the center of the skein with a square knot (see "Basics" and photo j).

❸ String a crimp bead and 24 beads on a 10-in. (25cm) length of flexible beading wire and go back through the crimp bead. String 72 beads, go back through the crimp bead, and pass each tail through a few more beads (photo k).

❹ Crimp the crimp bead (see "Basics") and trim the tails.

❺ Slide the tied bundle of floss through the small beaded loop. Center the floss in the loop and fold it so the knot is hidden in the fold. Pull the large loop up through the beaded tassel cover (photo l). About ½ in. (1.3cm) of floss should show above the tassel cover.

❻ Thread a needle and secure the tassel cover to the tassel by passing the needle back and forth through the peyote tube and tassel (photo m).

Hide the thread between the beads and repeat until the tassel cover stays in place.

❼ Wrap a strip of paper around the bottom of the tassel and use it as a guide to trim the floss evenly.
– June Huber

MATERIALS

- 3g size 11º Japanese cylinder beads, each of three colors
- crimp bead
- skein of embroidery floss
- 10 in. (25 cm) flexible beading wire, .014
- beading needles, #12
- Nymo B beading thread or Fireline fishing line, 6-lb. test
- beeswax or Thread Heaven for Nymo

Tools: crimping pliers

Optional: 18 3mm beads or small drops

Freeform
peyote vase

Sculptural peyote, making use of varying sizes and shapes of seed beads, can produce special results, as shown here in this stunning vase. Using seed beads of varying size and shape (6º–11º) allows for an unpredictable texture of lovely bumps and divots that produces an overall cohesive form. Try to avoid using beads with sharp edges that are likely to cut the thread, creating disasters and the need for tricky and immediate repairs.

CHOOSING COLORS

The vase pictured on pages 85 and 87 is done in a mostly warm palette. Red, gold, copper, and bronze beads contrast with neutral cream and black beads. Splashes of green and purple give the piece character and to make it more striking. For the piece shown in the process photos, three color families were chosen: purples and greens, secondary colors that share the primary color blue, and a neutral palette of ivories and golds.

Beading over clear glass allows light to pass through the transparent beads and adds an additional dimension of color and texture. It also means that thread is more likely to show, so be sure to choose a neutral (ash, gray, or taupe) that disappears into most of the bead colors. Beading over a gilded ceramic vase, as in the process piece, prevents full transparency of the beads, but it adds a reflective quality to the light that passes through the transparent beads. It also hides the thread because the gold dominates where thread might show.

GETTING STARTED

When beading over a shapely form, it is best to start around the narrowest part. I began this vase at the neck, stringing enough beads to encircle it and tying the thread together in a circle with about two to three beads worth of slack. I used a surgeon's knot (see "Basics," p. 5) and went through the first bead again to begin the peyote row. Since I would be using a variety of bead sizes throughout the project, I strung variously sized beads for the starting circle **(photo a)**. It's important to choose the right combination of bead colors and sizes to establish the

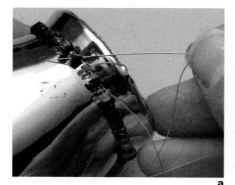

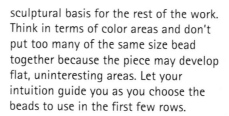

sculptural basis for the rest of the work. Think in terms of color areas and don't put too many of the same size bead together because the piece may develop flat, uninteresting areas. Let your intuition guide you as you choose the beads to use in the first few rows.

CHOOSING BEADS

A sculptural peyote piece deserves concern over just the right choice of bead. Because of the range of bead sizes and shapes in such a project, a miscalculation can cause the tension to look off. I've learned that patience helps you fill those tricky spaces. A sculptural piece requires unhurried choices, a little calculation, and a lot of intuition. Remember, the goal is an abstract but cohesive design.

As you peyote stitch around the form, you must increase and decrease,

depending on the form's shape. The smoother the shape, the more gradual your increases and decreases will be. You'll find that most of the increasing or decreasing will occur naturally as you bead. When the form swells, you'll use larger beads more frequently **(photo b)**, or you'll find yourself picking up two beads for a space where you would normally place one bead.

MATERIALS

- glass or ceramic vase with appealing shape
- variety of small beads in coordinating colors including 11º, 10º, 8º, 6º seed beads; triangle beads and square beads (approx. 3mm); niblets; 3-4mm crystals optional
- beading needles, #12 or 13
- Silamide or Nymo D beading thread in a neutral color (gray, ash, or beige)
- beeswax or Thread Heaven for Nymo

You may often find yourself doing two-drop peyote in the sections where you have picked up two beads. In other words, you go through two beads, pick up two beads, skip two beads, and go through two beads (continuing two drop peyote) or go through one bead, reverting to single peyote (photo c). To decrease (see "Basics"), you'll either use smaller beads or go through two beads as if they were one bead. When you come back to that spot, you'll pick up one bead to place over the two beads (photo d).

You'll find that when you pick up an especially large bead, a 6º or a niblet (a flat rectangle), you may have to go through that bead on several successive rows until the beadwork on either side of it is tall enough that you can cross over the top of the bead with the next row. For the beads on the row above a niblet, I often pick up an 11º, an 8º, and an 11º (photo e). Then on the next row, I pick up a bead above the first 11º, go through the 8º, and pick up a bead above the second 11º to resume regular peyote stitch.

BEADING THE LIP AND BASE

Beading with differently sized beads creates an uneven edge. As you near the edge of the rim and the bottom of the vase, pass through beads that extend especially close to the edge of the piece and build out the more distant sections (photo f). The goal is to have the final row end one 11º bead beyond the edge. Work one to three more rows to mask the edge completely; a few decreases are needed as the circle becomes smaller. End by passing the needle through all the beads of the last two rows once or twice to lessen the jaggedness of the edge and strengthen it.

The most dramatic decreasing occurs on the bottom of the vase. Keep the tension tight and consistent. I use only 11º beads on the bottom so the vase will sit flat. Because the size of the beads used previously has varied, it may be difficult to work evenly-spaced decreases around the bottom circle. You may have to decrease as needed when the beadwork begins to bulge. At first you'll decrease every other row or every third row. As you near the center of the bottom, you will probably have to decrease on every row. At the center, you'll have a small circle of beads (photo g). Pass the needle through all the beads twice and pull the circle snug. Weave in the thread and clip.
– *Fran Morris Mandel*

Spiral vessels

The spiral is an image that has fascinated humans since Paleolithic times, and it appears in the artwork of civilizations throughout the world. In nature, the spiral exemplifies the ratio known as the Golden Mean, a long-established formula for harmony and beauty.

These instructions contain the techniques, not the specific directions, for making a spiral vessel. The colors, proportions, and finished shape are for you to determine. As you stitch the walls of the vessel, you can bring the form inward, then let it surge out into a ruffle. You can build a rounded base that narrows to a slender neck. Leave the form open, as in the vessel shown below, or close it up, like the one opposite. Another alternative is to vary your bead sizes and shapes. Try working with size 11°s and small triangles or size 8°s and large ones.

Play with the colors to see how your selections look next to each other. Try rearranging types of beads until you have the sequence you like most, then lay them out so they'll end up in that order in your vessel.

❶ Arrange your beads in two rows with six piles of beads in each row, following the key of bead types in **figure 1**. Assign the 6º beads that you've chosen as the dominant color bands to numbers 2, 6, and 10. Assign the cube beads to numbers 3, 7, and 11. Cubes and beads assigned to numbers 1, 5, and 9 tend to stay in a single line. Number each pile so you don't lose track.

❷ Thread a needle onto approximately 5 yd. (4.5m) of Nymo. Work with the thread doubled. Don't knot the tails.
Row 1 Pick up one bead from color 1 (C1), color 5 (C5), and color 9 (C9) and slide them about 4 in. (10cm) from the tail ends. Go through these three beads again in the same direction. Tighten the thread so the beads form a triangle and go through them once more, exiting through C1 **(figure 2, a–b and photo a)**.
Row 2 Working in flat, circular peyote (also known as gourd) stitch (see "Basics," p. 5), increase as follows: Pick up one bead from C1 and C3. Go through the next bead. Pick up one bead from C5 and C7, go through the next bead. Pick up one bead from C9 and C11, and step up to start the next row **(figure 2, b–c and photo b)**. Step up at the beginning of each new row by going through the first bead of the previous row and the first bead of the row just completed.
Row 3 Pick up one bead after each bead in row 2. Match the bead you pick up to the bead your thread is exiting. **(figure 2, c–d and photo c)**. This is called a radical increase. Step up to the next row.
Row 4 Pick up two beads after each bead in row 3 as follows: C1 and C2, C3 and C4, C5 and C6, C7 and C8, C9 and C10, C11 and C12. Step up **(figure 2, d–e)**.
Rows 5 and 6 Pick up a bead after each bead in the previous row. Match the bead you pick up to the bead your thread is exiting. Step up after each row **(figure 2, e–f)**.
Row 7 Pick up a bead after each bead in the previous row as follows: (note the increases) one C1, two C2s, one C3, one C4, one C5, two C6s, one C7, one C8, one C9, two C10s, one C11, one C12. Step up **(figure 2, f–g)**.
Row 8 Pick up a bead after each bead

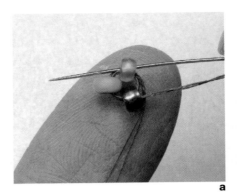

a

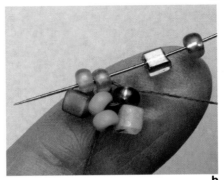

b

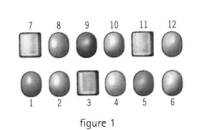

c

figure 1

in the previous row, matching the bead you pick up to the bead your thread is exiting. When you come to the row 7 increases in C2, C6, and C10, add a bead between the two beads (radical increase). Step up **(figure 2, g–h)**.
Row 9 Pick up a bead after each bead in the previous row as follows: (note the increases) one C1, two C2s, two C2s, one C3, one C4, one C5, two C6s, two C6s, one C7, one C8, one C9, two C10s, two C10s, one C11, one C12. Step up **(figure 2, h–i)**.
Row 10 Pick up a bead after each bead in the previous row (including increases) as in row 8. Step up **(figure 2, i–j)**.
Row 11 Pick up a bead after each bead in the previous row as in row 10. Step up **(figure 2, j–k)**.
Row 12 Pick up a bead after each bead in the previous row as in row 11. If your beads show a wide gap or if you want to expand the circumference, make a two-bead increase when you reach the second stitch of C2, C6, and C10. Step up.
Row 13 Pick up a bead after each bead in the previous row. If you increased in row 12, add beads between the two as in row 8. Step up.
Rows 14 and 15 Pick up a bead after each bead in the previous row. Tighten the thread tension and pull the beads upward to begin shaping the vessel

walls; or, to increase the circumference, make two-bead increases as in row 12.
Rows 16 to end The vessels shown here have approximately 50-65 rows. The increases and decreases you make in these rows determine the vessel's finished profile.

You can keep these changes within colors 2, 6, and 10, as in the blue vessel on p. 89, or play with increases (and later decreases) in other color bands. The walls curve outward when you increase. You control the extent of the bulging by the frequency and placement of additional beads. Remember to work a radical increase as in row 3 when you stitch the next row.

To bring the walls inward, decrease over two or four rows as follows, keeping the tension very tight.
First decrease row: Go through the next bead along the row without adding a bead before it **(photo d)**.
Second and third rows: When you come to the decrease, place one or two beads in the gap **(photo e)**. If you added one bead, the decrease is complete. If you added two beads, treat them as one when you stitch the third row **(photo f)**.
Fourth row: Place one bead over those two beads and continue **(photo g)**.
– Wendy Ellsworth

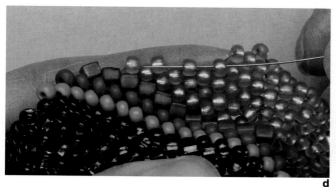

d

f

e

g

MATERIALS

- size 6º seed beads, 5g each of six colors
- size 6º seed beads, 36g each of
  three colors
- 4mm cube beads, 5g each of three colors
- Nymo D or F beading thread to match
  majority of bead colors
- beading needles, #10

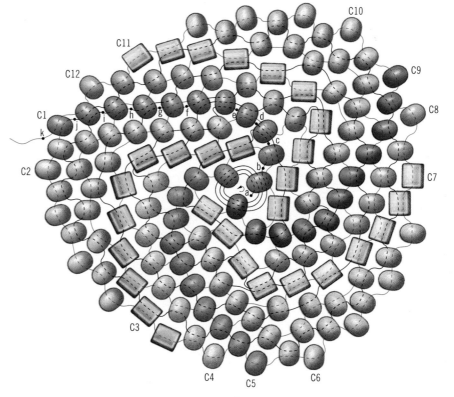

figure 2

Breathtaking ornaments

Christmas has always been a favorite holiday for Karen Boylan and her family. Each year, family and friends challenge her to create unusual tree settings and ornaments. In earlier years, with less time to be creative, she dressed up old scarred ornaments with glitter, ribbon, and old pieces of jewelry. It seemed natural to add strips of peyote stitch, sparkling beads, and crystals. The last twelve years of her forty years of beadweaving have produced the best compliment of all—a big smile when someone receives an ornament. What could be more satisfying?

The following instructions are for making the burgundy ornament pictured below. An understanding of peyote stitch is necessary to make this ornament. If you are new to this stitch, practice both odd- and even-count peyote, including increasing and decreasing before beginning (see "Basics," p. 5).

❶ String one gold bead onto 1 yd. (.9m) of Nymo to begin the collar for the ornament's cap. Go through the bead again. String one gold bead, four burgundy beads, and one gold bead for a total of six beads. Work in flat peyote

stitch for a total of 68 rows, working the edges in gold. Check the fit around the cap and add or remove rows if necessary. Make sure the total number of rows is an even number.

❷ Zigzag the collar ends together (photo a, p. 93). To secure, weave through the beads several times. Trim.

❸ To weave a side strip, string 58 burgundy beads on 1 yd. of thread. Work in flat peyote, with burgundy beads, following figure 1, p. 94. After working one side of the strip in gold beads, stitch over to the other side and work the gold beads on it. Make six strips.

❹ Note: It's easier to sew the strips onto the collar if you remove it from the globe. Position the end of one of the strips at the base of the collar. Weave the strip and the collar together securely by zigzagging back and forth through two edge beads per zigzag, one on each piece (photo b). Attach the remaining five strips to the collar, spacing them evenly (photo c).

❺ Attach 2 yd. (1.8m) of Nymo to one strip and come out the bottom right side's gold bead. String three burgundy and two gold beads. Add one gold bead and work in flat peyote stitch (figure 2, p. 94). At the end of the row, go through the first bead on the strip, then through the second strip bead to start the next row (figure 3, p. 94). Continue adding rows of peyote, following the charts and decreasing one gold bead at the edge in rows 4 and 5 (figures 4–5, p. 94). Continue working peyote but without attaching to a strip (figure 6, p. 94). After six rows, decrease one gold bead on the edge (figure 7, p. 94). After six more rows, connect to another strip. Continue around, connecting all

a

e

i

b

f

j

c

g

k

d

h

l

but one strip to the circle. Place the collar on the ornament and connect the last strip (photo d).

❻ Attach thread to the collar's top edge, exiting the top of a gold bead. Work a peyote strip across the cap's top, connecting to the collar's opposite edge. Continue adding rows, decreasing as needed, to cover the top with burgundy beads (photo e).

❼ Set the globe aside. Make the leaves, small petals, and large petals, following the instructions below.

LEAVES

❶ String 13 gold beads onto 6 in. (15.2cm) of 34-gauge wire. Bring the two ends of the wire together, forming a U. Twist the wire ends together at the base of the beads to form a leaf (photo f). Make 19 leaves.

❷ Twist the bottom of three leaves together (photo g). Position two more leaves slightly below the first three, twist all together. Add two more leaves three more times for a total of eleven, twisting them together to form a branch (photo h).

❸ Make another leaf formation with the remaining eight leaves.

LARGE FLOWER PETALS

If you're using the beads listed above, the following directions should work. However, you might need to alter the bead counts to suit your beads and the shape of the flower petal.

❶ String 30 burgundy beads onto 8 in. (20cm) of wire. Bring the ends together and twist to form an oval (photo i). With 2 ft. (61cm) of Nymo, go through all the oval beads, beginning at the twist

figure 1

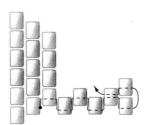

figure 2

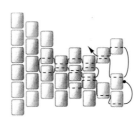

figure 4

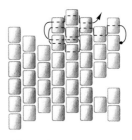

figure 6

figure 3

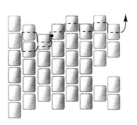

figure 5

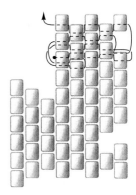

figure 7

MATERIALS

- 2½ in. (6.4cm) transparent globe
- Japanese cylinder beads, burgundy and gold, Delica #105 and 42
- 2.5 x 6.5mm gold rice-shaped beads
- Nymo B or D beading thread
- beading needles, #13
- 1 yd. burgundy ribbon, ⁵⁄₁₆ in. wide
- 34-gauge gold craft wire

Tools: hot glue gun

and leaving a 4-in. (10cm) tail. When you reach the twist, knot.

❷ String one gold rice bead and four gold beads. Go around the wire between the beads at top center and through the last bead added (photo j, p. 93). Work peyote stitch across the strand. When you reach the rice bead, go through it and around the wire. String four gold beads and go through the first gold bead after the rice bead. Continue working peyote stitch to the edge, decreasing if needed. Go around the wire and back through the last bead added on the previous row. Continue

working peyote stitch, decreasing as needed until you reach the side.

❸ Weave over to the other side and fill it in as in step 2 (photo k, p. 93). Go through three outer beads, knot around the wire, repeat, and trim. Secure the tail the same way. Make four more petals. Twist the petals together in a flower shape.

SMALL FLOWER PETALS

❶ Starting with 8 in. of wire, string 19 burgundy beads. Bring the ends together and twist at the beads, forming an oval. With 1½ ft. (46cm) of Nymo, go through the oval, beginning at the twist. Knot at the twist.

❷ String four gold and two burgundy beads. Go around the wire and through the last bead added. String a burgundy bead and peyote stitch; finish the row with gold beads. Go around the wire and continue working peyote stitch to the side, using gold beads and decreasing as needed. Weave over to the other side and fill in this section. Make two more small petals. Twist the petals together.

FINISHING

Position the leaves and small and large petals through the wire hanger (photo l, p. 93). Hot glue in place. Make a bow with the ribbon, tie to the hanger and hot glue. Tie the ends together, forming a hanger loop. – Karen Boylan

CONTRIBUTORS

Mary Lou Allen is a Wisconsin beader who focuses on form and shape using armatures and experimental loomwork. She also writes articles about jewelry-making. Contact her at 720 N. Duluth Ave., Sturgeon Bay, WI 54235, (970) 743-7313, beachstones1@charter.net.

Diane Benton teaches beading classes in Santa Barbara. Contact her at 816 E. Monticito St., Santa Barbara, CA 93103, (805) 705-6321, grayziggy@aol.com.

Karen Boylan is a prolific beader whose current projects include ornaments, jewelry, and lots of beaded handbags, like that shown on p. 10. Contact her at 3563 NW McCready, Bend, OR 97701.

Robin Brisco makes and designs wearable art. She lives in California.

Nicole Campanella is a frequent contributor to several jewelry magazines. Visit her website, nicolecampanella.com, to read about her beaded gourd contest and her new book. Contact her at beadwright@nicolecampanella.com.

David Chatt is an award-winning bead artist. See his website, davidchatt.com, to see more of his work.

Jennifer Clement is co-owner of Beadweaver in Santa Fe. Contact her at 503 Old Santa Fe Trail, NM 87505, (505) 955-1600, rbutterfly@earthlink.net.

Elisa Cossey is a Senior Teacher for PMC Connection and teaches beginning through Level II certification classes. Reach her at 2339 County St. 2940, Blanchard, OK 73010, elisa@silversunsetdesign.com. Visit her website, silversunsetdesign.com, to see more of her work.

Rev. Wendy Ellsworth teaches beading to Maasai and Samburu women in Kenya through Beads for Education (beadsforeducation.org). She is also working on a book about her journey with beads. Visit her website, ellsworthstudios.com, to see more of her work. Email her at davidellsworth@nni.com.

Janet Flynn is a bead artist living in the Washington, D.C. area. She writes, exhibits, and teaches nationwide. Contact her at 833 Walker Road, Great Falls, VA 22066, (703) 759-2529, janet@janetflynn.com. Visit her website, janetflynn.com, to see more of her work.

Barbara L. Grainger is a bead artist and author of three beading books. Visit her homepage, hometown.aol.com/bead-teach/Barbspage.html to learn more. Email her at beadteach@aol.com.

June Huber continues to work on new designs and teaches beading both nationally and in the Houston area. Email her at hubers@swbell.net.

Wendy Hubick and **Sue Jackson** are sisters who teach beadwork across the country. Visit their website, hummingbeads.com, to see more of their work. Email them at info@hummingbeads.com.

Kay A. Hutchison teaches bead classes at Beading Basics and The Bead Nest in Yuma, Arizona. Contact her at 3658 S. 10th Ave., Yuma, AZ 85365, (928) 314-4638.

Samantha Lynn is a Chicago-based writer currently trying to sell her first novel and working on a second. She blogs her adventures at livejournal.com/users/robling_t/. Contact her at samantha.lynn@sbcglobal.net.

Sharri Moroshok lives in Tallahassee, Florida. She has an extensive line of beaded bead kits that are available on her website, beadedbeads.com. Email her at sharri@beadedbeads.com.

Fran Morris Mandel loves to try new techniques and projects. She is currently working on tiny amulet purse centerpieces as well as a series of beaded pens and makeup brushes. A full-time graduate student, she somehow always manages to make time for her beading projects. Email her at franvmorris@yahoo.com.

Kelly Nicodemus-Miller operates a shop featuring her jewelry as well as that of 18 other designers and artists. Visit her website, krellydesigns.com to see more of her work. Contact her at Krelly Designs & Co., 1050 SW Baseline St. Suite A-5, Hillsboro, OR 97123, (503) 640-9434, krelly.designs@verizon.net.

Rebecca Peapples lives and beads in Michigan. Contact her at rspeapples@aol.com.

Debbie Phillips has been beading for more than 40 years and continues to share her love of beading by teaching classes. Contact her at 15 Fernwood Ct., Cary, IL 60013, (847) 516-3837, frank.a.phillips@mindspring.com.

Shantasa Saling lives in California. Visit her website, shantasa.com, to see more of her work. Email her at shantasa@msn.com.

Deb Samuels lives in Catskill, NY. Email her at debsamuels@yahoo.com.

Nicolette Stessin is the owner of Beadworld in Seattle. Contact her at 9520 Roosevelt Way NE, Seattle, WA 98115, (206) 523-0530.

Sue Swanson, MDiv, is a teacher and retreat leader who helps people find Sabbath time in their busy lives. Email her at swansonMN4@aol.com.

Cheri Lynn Waltz teaches beading classes at The Shepherdess in San Diego.

Rae Ann Wojahn has recently been experimenting with various freeform peyote projects. She lives with her husband, two children, and their cat, Spot, in the Northwest. Email her at rawojo@juno.com.

INDEX